Arthur Henry Bullen

Musa Proterva

Love-Poems of the Restoration

Arthur Henry Bullen

Musa Proterva
Love-Poems of the Restoration

ISBN/EAN: 9783744714068

Printed in Europe, USA, Canada, Australia, Japan

Cover: Foto ©Thomas Meinert / pixelio.de

More available books at **www.hansebooks.com**

MUSA PROTERVA:

LOVE-POEMS OF THE
RESTORATION.

EDITED BY
A. H. BULLEN.

LONDON:
PRIVATELY PRINTED.
1889.

PREFACE.

THE poems in my anthology *Speculum Amantis* belonged, with few exceptions, to the first half of the seventeenth century. In the present volume I have attempted to deal with the love-poetry of the Restoration and Revolution.

Manners were loose in the days of "old Rowley," and poets too frequently indulged in ribaldry.[1] No sensible reader will tolerate the foul and tedious grossness of the abandoned Rochester; and the obscenities of Restoration Drolleries have no place in honest literature. Who would care to watch a crew of goldfinders dancing round the shrine of Venus Cloacina? By all means let us shun such unedifying spectacles; but we need not wrap a thick cloak of prudishness about us and put on

---

[1] Professor Alexandre Beljame, in the early chapters of his learned and valuable work *Le Public et les Hommes de Lettres en Angleterre au Dix-huitième Siècle*, discusses this subject very fully.

a vinegar aspect. I like to see the Muse in good humour. Prior's lightest verses do not offend me, and I am enlivened by Sedley's gaiety. A few of the poems here collected may occasionally pass the bounds of strict decorum; but it will be found that these delinquencies (never of a violent character) are atoned by some happy jerk of fancy or playful sally of wit.

The Restoration was not one of the great ages of English poetry. Even in the poorest of Elizabethan dramatists and lyrists we find flashes of Shakespearean imagination, stray breaths of divine harmony, touches of romantic tenderness. But one may read Shadwell's plays (and they are well worth reading) from end to end without once catching a note of higher poetry. Shadwell is thoroughly representative of his age; he was the Ben Jonson of the Restoration,—Jonson stripped of his graces. Of the noble dramatists—"the giant race before the flood"—Shirley alone survived. Oldys tells how "young persons of parts" used to resort to Chapman in his declining days "as a poetical chronicle"; but no such homage was paid to Shirley by the wits of the Restoration. The author of *The Lady of Pleasure* and *The*

Grateful Servant, *The Cardinal* and *The Traitor*, would surely in any generous age have won the respect and gratitude of younger aspirants to fame, but Shirley at the end of his honourable career had to encounter neglect and contumely.

There was a dash of vulgarity, an absence of refinement and romance, in the dissipation of the king and his courtiers. In such uncongenial soil the rarer flowers of poetry could not take root. The finest poem in the present collection is Andrew Marvell's "Address to his Coy Mistress." There we have the clear spirit of poetry !—

> . . . "But at my back I always hear
> Time's winged chariot hurrying near,
> And yonder all before us lie
> Deserts of vast eternity." . . .

This is hardly the strain in which the Court poets wooed their mistresses. Marvell, the friend of Milton, was a rare visitor at Court.

Cowley does not come within our scope, for "The Mistress" was published in 1645. It is said that in later life he showed "an aversion to the company of women"; he did indeed pay (in 1664) a poetical tribute to the memory of Katherine Philips, the matchless Orinda, but long before the

Restoration he had ceased to write love-poetry. Waller, who died in 1687 at the ripe age of eighty-two, was regarded in Charles II.'s time and for many years afterwards as the master of harmonious numbers, the refiner of English speech, the Phœnix of politeness. "His compositions," wrote Gerard Langbaine in 1690, "are universally applauded; and they are thought fit to serve as a standard for all succeeding Poems." He is only now recovering from the damage inflicted on his reputation by such extravagant eulogy. His happiest lyrics were written in the days of Charles I.; but the tone and temper of his poetry connect him rather with the writers of the Restoration than with Suckling or Randolph. For chronological reasons I have reluctantly excluded him from my anthology.

Flatman and Charles Cotton are not seen to best advantage in their love-poetry. I have a great liking for both, and heartily regret that the former bore so unfortunate a name. Undoubtedly Flatman was a man of genius. His miniatures, though they are inferior at all points to Cooper's matchless masterpieces, are often singularly attractive, and his verses in praise of Faithorne are a splendid tribute to the worth of that distinguished master; but the fine and solemn poems inspired by his meditations on death constitute his chief claim to remembrance. Nahum Tate was a fervent admirer of Flatman; both were serious-minded poets (if Tate may be reckoned among the poets) in an age of frivolity. Charles Cotton's accomplishments were many and varied. He could throw a fly with any man in Christendom; he was a recognized authority on gardening; he made an excellent translation of Montaigne; he wrote that most entertaining and ingenious treatise *The Compleat Gamester*; and he keenly appreciated the virtues of nut-brown ale. His creditors harried him, and, to escape their importunity, he had often to fly from his house at Beresford and take refuge in a cave beside the Dove. But, in debt or in drink, he was always "honest cheerful Master Cotton." His poems addressed to Izaak Walton, and his ode on Winter, are not likely to be lightly forgotten. Here was a man of parts, a free frank jovial spirit, a boon-companion, a scholar, and a poet!

Sir William Davenant continued his literary activity to the end of his days. Born in 1605, he had been a copious writer for the stage in the reign of Charles I. An ardent loyalist, he had suffered some inconveniences—in the way of imprisonment—at the hands of the Parliamentarians. Much of his time was spent in France, where he had the misfortune to lose his nose. His briskness astonished younger men. "I found him," said Dryden, "of so quick a fancy that nothing was proposed to him on which he could not suddenly produce a thought extremely pleasant and surprising." On Restoration literature his influence was considerable.[1]

The songs in Dryden's plays are cheerful and sprightly. In the higher graces of poetry they are infinitely inferior to Fletcher's, but they are very good of their kind. With all his consummate genius Dryden could not reproduce such strains as "Lay a garland on my hearse" or "God Lyæus ever young." Mrs. Behn, the divine Astræa, was undoubtedly possessed of lyrical skill. The famous "Love in fantastic triumph sate" has been justly admired by a host of critics; but equally admirable is her impassioned song in praise of

---

[1] The best account of Davenant is to be found in Mr. Joseph Knight's admirable article contributed to the *Dictionary of National Biography*.

Love, "O Love, that stronger art than wine."[1] One of the lightest and happiest lyrists of the Restoration was Charles Sackville, Earl of Dorset. His song written at sea the night before an engagement,[2] "To all you ladies now at land," was very popular and provoked many imitations and parodies. He was the early patron of Prior, who attributed to him more virtues and talents than were ever centred in a single individual since the world began.

[1] But did Mrs. Behn write these fine verses? They first appeared in her comedy *The Lucky Chance*, 1687. Henry Playford, a well-known publisher of music, issued in the same year the Fourth Book of *The Theater of Music*, where "O Love, that stronger art" appeared with the heading "The Song in Madam Bhen's last new Play, sung by Mr. Bowman, set by Dr. John Blow." At the end of the song Playford adds, "These words by Mr. Ousley." It is possible that Playford was misinformed; but playwrights were in the habit of introducing songs written by their friends (frequently by some "person of quality"). Mrs. Behn usually acknowledges her obligations; but she may have been neglectful on the present occasion. Ousley's claim cannot be lightly set aside.

[2] "I have heard," says Dr. Johnson, "from the late Earl of Orrery, who was likely to have good hereditary intelligence, that Lord Buckhurst had been a week employed upon it, and only retouched or finished it on the memorable evening. But even this, whatever it may subtract from his facility, leaves him his courage."

Some specimens of the abilities of genial Tom Durfey have, of course, been included. Superfine critics sneer at honest Tom, but the gay rollicking ballad "The Winchester Wedding" will survive the assaults of these worthies. In his lifetime Durfey was attacked with spiteful virulence by Tom Brown, but he did not allow himself to be disconcerted by the snarls and snaps of that malicious creature. Of late he has found a stalwart champion in the person of the Rev. J. W. Ebsworth, editor of *The Roxburghe Ballads*, who has sounded his praises in prose and verse. Tom Brown hardly deserves a place in my anthology; but I have found room for one copy of verses—a clever imitation of one of Martial's epigrams.

John Oldmixon, the pamphleteer, was a waspish person. He was continually attacking somebody, and even ventured to have his fling at Pope, who promptly gibbeted him in *The Dunciad*. As he was universally disliked, his verses were usually kept out of the miscellanies of the time; but from his little volume of poems in the manner of Anacreon, published in 1696, I have chosen some dainty trifles.

I have stopped at the last decade of the seventeenth century, though I should have liked to advance a little further. Of John Bancks (not the playwright), who trod in the steps of La Fontaine and Prior, it would have been pleasant to give some specimens; for his poems are somewhat scarce.[1]

From Sir Charles Sedley I have drawn very freely. In his own sphere Sedley is unapproachable; such songs as "Love still has something of

---

[1] The reader shall have a taste of Bancks' quality: the mirthful catastrophe must atone for the freedom of the writing.

"A FRAGMENT.

In Chloe's chamber she and I
Together sate, no creature nigh;
The time and place combined to move
A longing for the joys of love.
I sighed and kissed, and pressed her hand;
Did all to make her understand.
She, pretty, tender-hearted creature
Obeyed the dictates of good nature,
As far as modesty would let her:
A melting virgin seldom speaks
But with her breasts and eyes and cheeks:
Nor was it hard from these to find
That Chloe had—almost—a mind.
Thus far 'twas well; but, to proceed,
What should I do? Grow bold—I did.
At last she faltered 'What would'st have?'
'Your love,' said I, 'or else my grave.'

the sea" or "Phillis is my only joy" easily outdistance all rivals. He does not occupy an exalted place in English literature; but his seat is secure.

I need not enter into further particulars about the contents of this little volume. The reader must not expect to find poetry of the highest order; but if he can appreciate polished verse he will not be dissatisfied. We seldom leave, it is true, the region of conventionality. The groves

> 'Suppose it were the first,' quoth she,
> 'Could you for ever constant be?'
> 'For ever, Chloe, by those eyes,
> Those bubbies which do fall and rise,
> By all that's soft and all that's fair,
> By your whole sacred self, I swear.
> Your fondest wishes ne'er shall crave
> So constant, so complete a slave.'
> 'Damon, you know too well the art,'
> She sighing said, ' to reach my heart.
> Yet oh! I can't, I won't comply—
> Why will you press? dear Damon, why?'
>   Desunt cætera.

> *For Chloe, coming in one day,*
> *As on my desk the copy lay,—*
> *'What means this rhyming fool?' she cries,*
> *'Why, some folk may believe these lies!'*
> *So on the flame she threw the sheet;*
> *I burned my hand to save this bit."*

in which our Strephons and Chloes disport themselves are not the green pleasaunces that listened to the pipings of Nicholas Breton's *Passionate Shepherd*. Our Arcadia is in Hyde Park and the Mulberry Garden; our nymphs are modishly attired, and our love-sick swains are powdered beaux.

LIST OF AUTHORS.

	PAGE
Atterbury, Francis, Bishop of Rochester	117
Ayres, Philip	102-103
Behn, Aphara	50-56
Brome, Alexander	8-10
Brown, Tom	113-114
Cavendish, William, Duke of Newcastle	1
Congreve, William	105-107
Cotton, Charles	13-16
Davenant, Sir William	2-7
Dryden, John	20-30
Duffett, Thomas	95-98
Durfey, Thomas	57-66
Etherege, Sir George	45-49
Farquhar, George	127-128
Finch, Anne, Countess of Winchilsea	108
Flatman, Thomas	17-19
Granville, George, Lord Lansdowne	110-112
Howard, Hon. James	87

LIST OF AUTHORS.

	PAGE
Marvell, Andrew	10-13
Motteux, Peter Anthony	122-124
New Airs and Dialogues	98-100
Oldmixon, John	118-122
Otway, Thomas	91
Philips, Katherine	19-20
Playford, John (*Fifth Book of Choice Airs*)	101-102
Rymer, Thomas	125-127
Sackville, Charles, Earl of Dorset	30-40
Scroope, Sir Car	49-50
Sedley, Sir Charles	66-86
Shadwell, Thomas	88-90
Sheffield, John, Duke of Buckinghamshire	103-104
Southerne, Thomas	109
Tate, Nahum	92
Walsh, William	114-117
Westminster Drollery	93-94
Wharton, Anne, Marchioness of	100-101
Wilmot, John, Earl of Rochester	41-45
Wilson, John	107-108

INDEX OF FIRST LINES.

	PAGE
A thousand martyrs I have made (*Aphara Behn*)	52
After the pangs of a desperate lover (*Dryden*)	24
Ah, Chloris, that I now could sit (*Sedley*)	66
Ah, Chloris, 'tis time to disarm your bright eyes (*Charles Sackville, Earl of Dorset*)	39
Ah he who first found out the way (*Aphara Behn*)	54
Ah how sweet it is to love (*Dryden*)	20
All my past life is mine no more (*John Wilmot, Earl of Rochester*)	43
Amintas, I am come alone (*Sedley*)	76
As Amoret with Phillis sat (*Sir Car Scroope*)	49
As Chloris full of harmless thought (*John Wilmot, Earl of Rochester*)	44
At noon, in a sunshiny day (*Charles Sackville, Earl of Dorset*)	37
At Winchester was a wedding (*Durfey*)	57
Aurelia, art thou mad (*Sedley*)	69
Be not too proud, imperious dame (*Flatman*)	17
Before the youthful spring had dyed (*Duffett*)	95
Beneath a myrtle shade (*Dryden*)	25
Boasting fops, who court the fair (*Motteux*)	124
Cælia, too late you would repent (*Walsh*)	114
Calm was the even and clear was the sky (*Dryden*)	21

INDEX OF FIRST LINES.

	PAGE
Celimena, of my heart (*Dryden*)	22
Celinda, think not by disdain (*Sedley*)	70
Chloe's a nymph in flowery groves (*Durfey*)	62
Chloe's the wonder of her sex (*George Granville, Lord Lansdowne*)	111
Chloris, I cannot say your eyes (*Sedley*)	72
Come, Celia, let's agree at last (*John Sheffield, Duke of Buckinghamshire*)	104
Damon, if thou wilt believe me (*Sedley*)	81
Damon, if you'd have me true (*Aphara Behn*)	55
Distracted with care (*Walsh*)	115
Dorinda's sparkling wit and eyes (*Charles Sackville, Earl of Dorset*)	39
Fair Amoret is gone astray (*Congreve*)	106
Farewell, ungrateful traitor (*Dryden*)	29
Flavia the least and slightest toy (*Atterbury*)	117
Forbear, bold youth; all's heaven here (*Katherine Philips*)	19
Give me leave to rail at you (*John Wilmot, Earl of Rochester*)	42
Had we but world enough and time (*Marvell*)	10
How hardly I concealed my tears (*Anne, Marchioness of Wharton*)	100
I did but look and love a-while (*Otway*)	91
I followed fame and got renown (*Durfey*)	64
I love, but she alone shall know (*Motteux*)	123
I must confess I am untrue (*John Sheffield, Duke of Buckinghamshire*)	103
If she be not as kind as fair (*Etherege*)	45

INDEX OF FIRST LINES.

	PAGE
Impatient with desire, at last (*George Granville, Lord Lansdowne*)	111
In vain, Clemene, you bestow (*Charles Sackville, Earl of Dorset*)	40
It is not, Celia, in our power (*Etherege*)	47
Ladies, farewell, I must retire (*James Howard*)	87
Ladies, though to your conquering eyes (*Etherege*)	45
Late when Love I seemed to slight (*Rymer*)	126
Like a dog with a bottle fast tied to his tail (*Flatman*)	18
Love in fantastic triumph sate (*Aphara Behn*)	50
Love still has something of the sea (*Sedley*)	75
Love, when 'tis true, needs not the aid (*Sedley*)	85
Maids, beware! maids, beware! (*New Airs and Dialogues*)	100
Man is for the woman made (*Motteux*)	122
May the ambitious ever find (*Charles Sackville, Earl of Dorset*)	33
Methinks the poor town has been troubled too long (*Charles Sackville, Earl of Dorset*)	35
More love or more disdain I crave (*New Airs and Dialogues*)	98
My dear mistress has a heart (*John Wilmot, Earl of Rochester*)	41
My lodging is on the cold ground (*Davenant*)	2
Not, Cælia, that I juster am (*Sedley*)	73
Nymph Fanaret, the gentlest maid (*Nahum Tate*)	92
O happy flea, that may'st both kiss and bite (*Shadwell*)	88
O Love, that stronger art than wine (*Aphara Behn*)	51
O 'tis sweet, 'tis wondrous sweet (*Oldmixon*)	118
O what a pleasure 'tis to find (*Aphara Behn*)	53
Oh, how the hand the lover ought to prize (*Aphara Behn*)	56

	PAGE
Persuade me not there is a grace (*Anne Finch, Countess of Winchilsea*)	108
Phillis, I expect caresses (*Rymer*)	125
Phillis is my only joy (*Sedley*)	80
Phillis, let's shun the common fate (*Sedley*)	71
Phillis, men say that all my vows (*Sedley*)	68
Phillis, the fairest of Love's foes (*Charles Sackville, Earl of Dorset*)	34
Phillis, this early zeal assuage (*Sedley*)]	74
Pious Selinda goes to prayers (*Congreve*)	106
Preserve thy sighs, unthrifty girl (*Davenant*)	6
Prithee, Chloe, not so fast (*Oldmixon*)	119
Pursuing beauty, men descry (*Southerne*)	109
Smooth was the water, calm the air (*Sedley*)	79
So well Corinna likes the joy (*George Granville, Lord Lansdowne*)	112
Some thirty or forty or fifty at least (*Durfey*)	65
Still wilt thou sigh, and still in vain (*Shadwell*)	89
Sweet, use your time; abuse your time (*Durfey*)	65
Sweetest bud of beauty, may (*Etherege*)	46
Tell me, Jenny, tell me roundly (*John Playford's Fifth Book of Choice Airs*)	101
Tell me no more I am deceived (*Etherege*)	48
Tell me no more I am deceived (*Congreve*)	105
Tell me not of a face that's fair (*Alexander Brome*)	8
The day is come, I see it rise (*Dryden*)	28
The lark now leaves his wat'ry nest (*Davenant*)	6
The night her blackest sable wore (*Durfey*)	60
There's none so pretty (*Westminster Drollery*)	93
Think'st thou that this love can stand (*Marvell*)	12
Those arts which common beauties move (*Oldmixon*)	121
Thou fool! if madness be so rife (*Cotton*)	16

INDEX OF FIRST LINES.

	PAGE
Thus Damon knocked at Celia's door (*Farquhar*)	127
'Tis true I never was in love (*Alexander Brome*)	9
To all you ladies now at land (*Charles Sackville, Earl of Dorset*)	30
To charming Cælia's arms I flew (*Tom Brown*)	113
Was ever man of Nature's framing (*Cotton*)	13
Well-placed in Love's triumphant chariot high (*William Cavendish, Duke of Newcastle*)	1
Were I to take wife (*John Wilson*)	107
When, Cælia, must my old day set (*Cotton*)	14
When first I made love to my Chloris (*Sedley*)	84
When I a lover pale do see (*New Airs and Dialogues*)	99
When light begins the eastern heaven to grace (*Philip Ayres*)	102
When with Flavia I am toying (*Oldmixon*)	120
Whilst Alexis lay prest (*Dryden*)	26
Why, cruel creature, why so bent (*George Granville, Lord Lansdowne*)	110
Why dost thou seem to boast, vain-glorious sun (*Davenant*)	4
Young Corydon and Phillis (*Sedley*)	82
Young Philander wooed me long (*Durfey*)	63
Your beauty, ripe, and calm, and fresh (*Davenant*)	5

MUSA PROTERVA.

By William Cavendish,
Duke of Newcastle.
From *The Humorous Lovers*, 1677.

WELL-PLACED in Love's triumphant chariot high,
Be drawn with milk-white turtles through the sky,
And have for footmen Cupids running by.

A poet coachman with celestial fire,
His gentle whip of melting pure desire,
Shall drive us while I do thy eyes admire.

Imperial laurel deck our temples round,
As victors or as heated poets crowned,
Scorning to have commerce with the dull ground.

Thus we will drive o'er mighty hills of snow,
Viewing poor mortal lovers here below,
Wretches alas! that know not where we go.

From Sir William Davenant's *The Rivals*, 1668.

My lodging[1] is on the cold ground,
    And very hard is my fare,

---

[1] This song is parodied in Hon. James Howard's *All Mistaken, or the Mad Couple*, 1672. In *Speculum Amantis*, p. 89, I gave another song from *The Rivals*. I may find room in this footnote for an earlier love-song, taken from *The Triumphs of the Prince d'Amour*, 1635:—

"Unarm, unarm! no more your fights
    Must cause the virgins tears,
But such as in the silent nights
    Spring rather from their fears.

"Such diff'rence as when doves do bill
    Must now be all your strife;
For all the blood that you shall spill
    Will usher in a life.

"And when your ladies, falsely coy,
    Shall timorous appear,
Believe they then would fain enjoy
    What they pretend to fear.

"Breathe then each other's breath, and kiss
    Your souls to union;
And whilst they shall enjoy this bliss,
    Your bodies, too, are one.

"To-morrow will the hasty sun
    Be feared more of each lover
For hind'ring to repeat what's done
    Than what it may discover."

But that which troubles me most is
   The unkindness of my dear.
Yet still I cry, O turn, love,
   And I prithee, love, turn to me;
For thou art the man that I long for,
   And, alack! what remedy?

I'll crown thee with a garland of straw then,
   And I'll marry thee with a rush ring,
My frozen hopes shall thaw then,
   And merrily we will sing.
O turn to me, my dear love,
   And prithee, love, turn to me,
For thou art the man that alone canst
   Procure my liberty.

But, if thou wilt harden thy heart still
   And be deaf to my pitiful moan,
Then I must endure the smart still
   And tumble in straw alone:
Yet still I cry, O turn, love,
   And I prithee, love, turn to me,
For thou art the man that alone art
   The cause of my misery.

By Sir William Davenant.

Against Women's Pride.

WHY dost thou seem to boast, vain-glorious
    sun?
  Why should thy bright complexion make thee
    proud?
Think but how often since thy race begun
  Thou wert eclipsed, then blush behind a cloud!

Or why look you, fair Empress of the night,
  So big upon 't, when you at full appear?
Remember yours is but a borrowed light;
  Then shrink with paleness in your giddy sphere!

If neither sun nor moon can justify
  Their pride, how ill it women then befits,
That are on earth but *ignes fatui*,
  That lead poor men to wander from their wits!

By Sir William Davenant.

The Philosopher and the Lover; to a Mistress dying.

Lover.

YOUR beauty, ripe, and calm, and fresh,
    As eastern summers are,
Must now, forsaking time and flesh,
    Add light to some small star.

Philosopher. Whilst she yet lives, were stars decayed,
    Their light by hers relief might find;
But Death will lead her to a shade
    Where Love is cold and Beauty blind.

Lover. Lovers, whose priests all poets are,
    Think every mistress, when she dies,
Is changed at least into a star:
    And who dares doubt the poets wise?

Philosopher. But ask not bodies doomed to die
    To what abode they go;
Since Knowledge is but Sorrow's spy
    It is not safe to know.

By Sir William Davenant.

THE lark now leaves his wat'ry nest
   And, climbing, shakes his dewy wings;
He takes this window for the east,
   And to implore your light he sings:
Awake, awake! the morn will never rise
Till she can dress her beauty at your eyes.

The merchant bows unto the seaman's star,
   The ploughman from the sun his season takes;
But still the lover wonders what they are
   Who look for day before his mistress wakes.
Awake, awake! break through your veils of lawn,
Then draw your curtains and begin the dawn.

By Sir William Davenant.

The Soldier going to the Field.

PRESERVE thy sighs, unthrifty girl,
   To purify the air;
Thy tears to thread, instead of pearl,
   On bracelets of thy hair.

The trumpet makes the echo hoarse,
    And wakes the louder drum;
Expense of grief gains no remorse
    When sorrow should be dumb:

For I must go where lazy Peace
    Will hide her drowsy head,
And, for the sport of kings, increase
    The number of the dead.

But first I'll chide thy cruel theft:
    Can I in war delight
Who, being of my heart bereft,
    Can have no heart to fight?

Thou know'st the sacred laws of old
    Ordained a thief should pay,
To quit him of his theft, sevenfold
    What he had stol'n away.

Thy payment shall but double be:
    O then with speed resign
My own seduced heart to me
    Accompanied with thine.

By Alexander Brome.

THE RESOLVE.

TELL me not of a face that's fair,
    Nor lip and cheek that's red,
Nor of the tresses of her hair,
    Nor curls in order laid,
Nor of a rare seraphic voice
    That like an angel sings;
Though if I were to take my choice
    I would have all these things:
But if that thou wilt have me love,
    And it must be a she,
The only argument can move
    Is that she will love me.

The glories of your ladies be
    But metaphors of things,
And but resemble what we see
    Each common object brings.
Roses out-red their lips and cheeks,
    Lilies their whiteness stain:
What fool is he that shadows seeks
    And may the substance gain?

Then if thou'lt have me love a lass,
    Let it be one that's kind:
Else I'm a servant to the glass
    That's with Canary lined.

By ALEXANDER BROME.

A MOCK-SONG.

'TIS true I never was in love;
    But now I mean to be,
        For there's no art
        Can shield a heart
From love's supremacy.

Though in my nonage I have seen
    A world of taking faces,
I had not age nor wit to ken
    Their several hidden graces.

Those virtues which, though thinly set,
    In others are admired,
In thee are altogether met,
    Which make thee so desired;

> That, though I never was in love
> Nor never meant to be,
> Thy self and parts
> Above my arts
> Have drawn my heart to thee.

By ANDREW MARVELL.

TO HIS COY MISTRESS.

HAD we but world enough and time
This coyness, lady, were no crime.
We would sit down and think which way
To walk, and pass our long love's day.
Thou by the Indian Ganges' side
Shouldst rubies find: I by the tide
Of Humber would complain. I would
Love you ten years before the flood,
And you should, if you please, refuse
Till the conversion of the Jews.
My vegetable love should grow
Vaster than empires, and more slow;
An hundred years should go to praise
Thine eyes, and on thy forehead gaze;

Two hundred to adore each breast,
But thirty thousand to the rest;
An age at least to every part,
And the last age should show your heart;
For, lady, you deserve this state,
Nor would I love at lower rate.

But at my back I always hear
Time's winged chariot hurrying near;
And yonder all before us lie
Deserts of vast eternity.
Thy beauty shall no more be found,
Nor, in thy marble vault, shall sound
My echoing song: then worms shall try
That long preserved virginity,
And your quaint honour turn to dust,
And into ashes all my lust:
The grave's a fine and private place,
But none, I think, do there embrace.

Now therefore, while the youthful hue
Sits on thy skin like morning dew,
And while thy willing soul transpires
At every pore with instant fires,
Now let us sport us while we may,
And now, like amorous birds of prey,

Rather at once our time devour
Than languish in his slow-chapt[1] power.
Let us roll all our strength and all
Our sweetness up into one ball,
And tear our pleasures with rough strife
Thorough the iron gates of life:
Thus, though we cannot make our sun
Stand still, yet we will make him run.

By ANDREW MARVELL.

MAKING HAY-ROPES.

Ametas.

THINK'ST[2] thou that this love can stand,
  Whilst thou still dost say me nay?
Love unpaid does soon disband:
  Love binds love as hay binds hay.

Thestylis. Think'st thou that this rope would twine
  If we both should turn one way?
Where both parties so combine,
  Neither love will twist nor hay.

---

[1] "Slow-chapt"—with *chaps* (jaws) that slowly consume.

[2] Mr. W. J. Linton has some neatly-turned verses (headed "No Marvel") suggested by the present poem. See his *Poems and Translations*, p. 7.

Ametas. Thus you vain excuses find,
    Which yourself and us delay:
And love ties a woman's mind
    Looser than with ropes of hay.

Thestylis. What you cannot constant hope
    Must be taken as you may.
Ametas. Then let's both lay by our rope
    And go kiss within the hay.

By CHARLES COTTON.

WAS ever man of Nature's framing
    So given o'er to roving,
Who have been twenty years a-taming
By ways that are not worth the naming,
    And now must die of loving?

Hell take me if she ben't so winning
    That now I love her mainly!
And though in jest at the beginning,
Yet now I'd wondrous fain be sinning,
    And so have told her plainly.

At which she cries I do not love her,
  And tells me of her honour;
Then have I no way to disprove her,
And my true passion to discover,
  But straight to fall upon her.

Which done, forsooth, she talks of wedding,
  But what will that avail her?
For though I am old dog at bedding,
I'm yet a man of so much reading
  That there I sure shall fail her.

No, hang me if I ever marry
  Till womankind grow stauncher!
I do delight delights to vary,
And love not in one hulk to tarry,
  But only trim and launch her.

By CHARLES COTTON.

To Cælia.

WHEN, Cælia, must my old day set
  And my young morning rise,
In beams of joy so bright as yet
  Ne'er blessed a lover's eyes?

My state is more advanced than when
    I first attempted thee;
I sued to be a servant then,
    But now to be made free.

I've served my time faithful and true,
    Expecting to be placed
In happy freedom, as my due,
    To all the joys thou hast:
Ill husbandry in love is such
    A scandal to love's power,
We ought not to mis-spend so much
    As one poor short-lived hour.

Yet think not, sweet, I'm weary grown
    That I pretend such haste,
Since none to surfeit e'er was known
    Before he had a taste:
My infant love could humbly wait
    When young it scarce knew how
To plead; but, grown to man's estate,
    He is impatient now.

By CHARLES COTTON.

RONDEAU.

THOU fool! if madness be so rife
    That, spite of wit, thou'lt have a wife,
I'll tell thee what thou must expect,—
After the honey-moon neglect
All the sad days of thy whole life!

To that a world of woe and strife,
Which is of marriage the effect;
And thou thy own woe's architect,
              Thou fool!
Thou'lt nothing find but disrespect,
Ill words i' th' scolding dialect,
For she'll all tabor be or fife.
Then prithee go and whet thy knife,
And from this fate thyself protect,
              Thou fool!

By Thomas Flatman.

The Defiance.

BE not too proud, imperious dame;
    Your charms are transitory things
    May melt, while you at Heaven aim,
    Like Icarus' waxen wings;
And you a part in his misfortune bear,
Drowned in a briny ocean of despair.

    You think your beauties are above
    The poet's brain and painter's hand,
    As if upon the throne of love
    You only should the world command:
Yet know, though you presume your title true,
There are pretenders that will rival you.

    There's an experienced rebel Time,
    And in his squadron's Poverty;
    There's Age that brings along with him
    A terrible artillery:
And if against all those thou keep'st thy crown,
Th' usurper Death will make thee lay it down.

By Thomas Flatman.

The Bachelor's Song.

LIKE[1] a dog with a bottle fast tied to his tail,
Like vermin in a trap or a thief in a jail,
    Like a Tory in a bog
    Or an ape with a clog:
Such is the man who, when he might go free,
    Does his liberty lose
    For a matrimony noose,
And sells himself into captivity.
The dog he does howl when the bottle does jog;
The vermin, the thief, and the Tory in vain
Of the trap, of the jail, of the quagmire complain.
But well fare poor Pug! for he plays with his clog
And, though he would be rid on 't rather than his life,
Yet he lugs it and he hugs it as a man does his wife.

[1] Some waggish friends of Flatman sang this song beneath his window on his marriage-night. Anthony à Wood tells the story. In the *Westminster Drollery* we find some answers to "The Bachelor's Song," which was very popular.

The Second Part.

How happy a thing were a wedding,
                And a bedding,
If a man might purchase a wife
  For a twelve-month and a day!
But to live with her all a man's life
  For ever and for aye
Till she grow as grey as a cat,
Good faith, Mr. Parson, I thank you for that.

By KATHERINE PHILIPS (*the matchless* ORINDA).

AN ANSWER TO ANOTHER PERSUADING A LADY TO MARRIAGE.

FORBEAR, bold youth; all's heaven here,
  And what you do aver
To others courtship may appear;
  'Tis sacrilege to her.

She is a public deity;
  And were 't not very odd
She should dispose herself to be
  A petty household god.

First make the sun in private shine
    And bid the world adieu,
That so he may his beams confine
    In compliment to you:

But if of that you do despair,
    Think how you did amiss
To strive to fix her beams which are
    More bright and large than his.[1]

From JOHN DRYDEN's *Tyrannic Love*, 1670.

AH how sweet it is to love!
    Ah how gay is young desire!
And what pleasing pains we prove
When we first approach love's fire!
    Pains of love be sweeter far
    Than all other pleasures are.

Sighs which are from lovers blown
Do but gently heave the heart:
Ev'n the tears they shed alone,
Cure, like trickling balm, their smart:
    Lovers, when they lose their breath,
    Bleed away in easy death.

[1] Old ed. "this."

Love and time with reverence use,
Treat 'em like a parting friend;
Nor the golden gifts refuse
Which in youth sincere they send;
    For each year their price is more,
    And they less simple than before.

Love, like spring-tides full and high,
Swells in every youthful vein;
But each tide does less supply
Till they quite shrink in again :
    If a flow in Age appear,
    'Tis but rain, and runs not clear.

From JOHN DRYDEN'S *An Evening's Love*, 1671.

CALM was the even and clear was the sky,
    And the new-budding flowers did spring,
When all alone went Amyntas and I
    To hear the sweet nightingale sing.
I sat, and he laid him down by me,
    But scarcely his breath he could draw,
For when with a fear he began to draw near
    He was dashed with A ha, ha, ha, ha!

He blush'd to himself, and lay still for a while,
   And his modesty curbed his desire;
But straight I convinced all his fears with a smile,
   Which added new flames to his fire.
O Sylvia, said he, you are cruel
   To keep your poor lover in awe;
Then once more he prest with his hand to my breast,
   But was dashed with A ha, ha, ha, ha!

I knew 'twas his passion that caused all his fear,
   And therefore I pitied his case:
I whispered him softly "There's nobody near,"
   And laid my cheek close to his face:
But as he grew bolder and bolder,
   A shepherd came by us and saw,
And, just as our bliss we began with a kiss,
   He laughed out with A ha, ha, ha, ha!

Damon.

CELIMENA, of my heart
   None shall e'er bereave you;
If with your good leave I may
Quarrel with you once a day,
   I will never leave you.

Celim. Passion's but an empty name
    Where respect is wanting:
Damon, you mistake your aim:
Hang your heart and burn your flame,
    If you must be ranting.

Damon. Love as dull and muddy is
    As decaying liquor:
Anger sets it on the lees,
And refines it by degrees
    Till it works the quicker.

Celim. Love by quarrels to beget
    Wisely you endeavour,
With a grave physician's wit,
Who to cure an ague fit
    Put me in a fever.

Damon. Anger rouses love to fight
    And his only bait is;
'Tis the spur to dull delight,
And is but an eager bite
    When desire at height is.

Celim. If such drops of heat can fall
    In our wooing weather;

If such drops of heat can fall,
We shall have the devil and all
When we come together.

AFTER the pangs of a desperate lover,
When day and night I have sighed all in vain,
Ah what a pleasure it is to discover
In her eyes pity who causes my pain!

When with unkindness our love at a stand is,
And both have punished ourselves with the pain,
Ah what a pleasure the touch of her hand is,
Ah what a pleasure to press it again!

When the denial comes fainter and fainter,
And her eyes give what her tongue does deny,
Ah what a trembling I feel when I venture,
Ah what a trembling does usher my joy!

When with a sigh she accords me the blessing,
And her eyes twinkle 'twixt pleasure and pain,
Ah what a joy 'tis, beyond all expressing,
Ah what a joy to hear "Shall we again?"

From JOHN DRYDEN'S *The First Part of the Conquest of Granada*, 1672.

BENEATH a myrtle shade,
   Which Love for none but happy lovers made,
I slept; and straight my love before me brought
Phillis, the object of my waking thought:
Undressed she came my flames to meet,
While Love strowed flowers beneath her feet,
Flowers which, so pressed by her, became more
      sweet.

   From the bright vision's head
A careless veil of lawn was loosely spread:
From her white temples fell her shaded hair,
Like cloudy sunshine, not too brown nor fair;
Her hands, her lips did love inspire,
Her every grace my heart did fire:
But most her eyes, which languished with desire.

   Ah, charming fair, said I,
How long can you my bliss and yours deny?
By Nature and by Love this lonely shade
Was for revenge of suff'ring lovers made:

Silence and shades with love agree,
Both shelter you and favour me;
You cannot blush because I cannot see.

    No, let me die, she said,
Rather than lose the spotless name of maid:
Faintly, methought, she spoke, for all the while
She bid me not believe her with a smile.
Then die, said I. She still denied,
And is it thus, thus, thus, she cried,
You use a harmless maid? and so she died.

    I waked, and straight I knew
I loved so well it made my dream prove true:
Fancy, the kinder mistress of the two,
Fancy had done what Phillis would not do.
Ah cruel nymph, cease your disdain,
While I can dream you scorn in vain:
Asleep or waking you must ease my pain.

From JOHN DRYDEN's *Marriage-a-la-Mode*, 1673.

WHILST Alexis lay prest
    In her arms he loved best,
With his hand round her neck
And his head on her breast,

He found the fierce pleasure too hasty to stay,
And his soul in the tempest just flying away.

When Cælia saw this,
With a sigh and a kiss
She cried "Oh my dear, I am robbed of my bliss;
'Tis unkind to your love, and unfaithfully done,
To leave me behind you and die all alone."

The youth, tho' in haste
And breathing his last,
In pity died slowly while she died more fast,
Till at length she cried "Now, my dear, now let us
    go !
Now die, my Alexis, and I will die too."

Thus entranced they did lie,
Till Alexis did try
To recover new breath that again he might die :
Then often they died; but the more they did so,
The nymph died more quick and the shepherd
    more slow.

> From JOHN DRYDEN'S *Amboyna*, 1673.

THE day is come, I see it rise
  Betwixt the bride's and bridegroom's eyes,
That golden day they wished so long,
Love picked it out amidst the throng;
He destined to himself this sun,
And took the reins and drove him on;
In his own beams he dressed him bright,
Yet bid him bring a better night.

The day you wished arrived at last,
You wish as much that it were past;
One minute more and night will hide
The bridegroom and the blushing bride.
The virgin now to bed does go;
Take care, O youth, she rise not so;
She pants and trembles at her doom,
And fears and wishes thou wouldst come.

The bridegroom comes, he comes apace
With love and fury in his face;
She shrinks away, he close pursues,
And prayers and threats at once does use.

She, softly sighing, begs delay,
And with her hand puts his away:
Now out aloud for help she cries,
And now despairing shuts her eyes.

From JOHN DRYDEN'S *The Spanish Friar*, 1681.

FAREWELL, ungrateful traitor,
    Farewell, my perjured swain!
Let never injured creature
    Believe a man again.
The pleasure of possessing
Surpasses all expressing;
But 'tis too short a blessing,
    And love too long a pain.

'Tis easy to deceive us
    In pity of your pain;
But when we love you leave us
    To rail at you in vain.
Before we have descried it
There is no bliss beside it;
But she that once has tried it
    Will never love again.

The passion you pretended
  Was only to obtain;
But when the charm is ended
  The charmer you disdain.
Your love by ours we measure
Till we have lost our treasure;
But dying is a pleasure
  When living is a pain.

By CHARLES SACKVILLE, EARL
OF DORSET.

SONG; WRITTEN AT SEA IN THE FIRST DUTCH WAR, 1665, THE NIGHT BEFORE AN ENGAGEMENT.

TO all you ladies now at land
  We men at sea indite;
But first would have ye understand
  How hard it is to write:
The Muses now and Neptune, too,
We must implore to write to you.

For tho' the Muses should prove kind
  And fill our empty brain,
Yet, if rough Neptune call the wind
  To rouse the azure main,
Our paper, pen, and ink, and we
Roll up and down our ships at sea.

Then, if we write not by each post,
  Think not we are unkind,
Nor yet conclude our ships are lost
  By Dutchmen or by wind:
Our tears we'll send a speedier way,
The tide shall bring them twice a day.

The King, with wonder and surprise,
  Will swear the seas grow bold,
Because the tides will higher rise
  Than e'er they used of old:
But let him know it is our tears
Bring floods of grief to Whitehall stairs.

Should foggy Opdam chance to know
  Our sad and dismal story,
The Dutch would scorn so weak a foe
  And say they've gained no glory;
For what resistance can they find
From men who've left their hearts behind.

Let wind and weather do its worst,
   Be you to us but kind;
Let Dutchmen vapour, Spaniards curse,
   No sorrow we shall find:
'Tis then no matter how things go,
Or who's our friend, or who's our foe.

To pass our tedious hours away
   We throw a merry main,
Or else at serious ombre play;
   But why should we in vain
Each other's ruin thus pursue?
We were undone when we left you.

But now our fears tempestuous grow
   And cast our hopes away,
Whilst you, regardless of our woe,
   Sit careless at a play;
Perhaps permit some happier man
To kiss your hand or flirt your fan.

When any mournful tune you hear
   That dies in every note,
As if it sighed with each man's care
   For being so remote;
Think then how often love we've made
To you, when all those tunes were played.

In justice you cannot refuse
   To think of our distress,
When we for hopes of honour lose
   Our certain happiness;
All those designs are but to prove
Ourselves more worthy of your love.

And now we've told you all our loves,
   And likewise all our fears,
In hopes this declaration moves
   Some pity for our tears;
Let's hear of no inconstancy,
We have too much of that at sea.

By the EARL OF DORSET.

MAY the ambitious ever find
   Success in crowds and noise,
While gentler love does fill my mind
   With silent real joys!

May knaves and fools grow rich and great,
   And the world think them wise,
While I lie dying at her feet
   And all the world despise.

Let conquering kings new triumphs raise
    And melt in court delights;
Her eyes can give much brighter days,
    Her arms much softer nights.

By the Earl of Dorset.

PHILLIS, the fairest of Love's foes,
    Though fiercer than a dragon,
Phillis, that scorned the powdered beaux,
    What has she now to brag on?
So long she kept her legs so close
    Till she had scarce a rag on.

Compelled through want, this wretched maid
    Did sad complaints begin;
Which surly Strephon hearing said
    It was both shame and sin
To pity such a lazy jade
    As will neither play nor spin.

By the Earl of Dorset.

METHINKS the poor town has been troubled too long,
With Phillis and Chloris in every song,
By fools who at once can both love and despair
And will never leave calling them cruel and fair;
Which justly provokes me in rhyme to express
The truth that I know of bonny Black Bess.[1]

This Bess of my heart, this Bess of my soul,
Has a skin white as milk and hair black as a coal;
She's plump, yet with ease you may span round her waist,
But her round swelling thighs can scarce be embraced:
Her belly is soft, not a word of the rest,
But I know what I think when I drink to the best.

The plowman and squire, the arranter clown,
At home she subdued in her paragon gown;
But now she adorns both the boxes and pit,
And the proudest town-gallants are forced to submit;

[1] Horace Walpole, in his copy of *The Sports of the Muses*, 1752, preserved in the Dyce Library, notes that "Black Bess" was Mrs. Barnes.

All hearts fall a-leaping wherever she comes,
And beat day and night like my Lord Craven's [1]
    drums.

I dare not permit her to come to Whitehall,
For she'd outshine the ladies, paint, jewels, and all;
If a lord should but whisper his love in the crowd,
She'd sell him a bargain and laugh out aloud:
Then the Queen, overhearing what Betty did say,
Would send Mr. Roper [2] to take her away.

But to those that have had my dear Bess in their
    arms,
She's gentle, and knows how to soften her charms;
And to every beauty can add a new grace,
Having learned how to lisp and to trip in her pace;
And with head on one side, and a languishing eye,
To kill us by looking as if she would die.

---

[1] Pepys, in March, 1668, describes Lord Craven as "riding up and down to give orders like a madman" to the troops gathered in Lincoln's Inn Fields for the suppression of a city tumult. Whenever a fire broke out Lord Craven was very active; his horse could scent fire at a distance.

[2] Christopher Roper, appointed page of honour to the Queen in 1667.

By the Earl of Dorset.

A T noon, in a sunshiny day,
　　The brightest lady of the May,
Young Chloris, innocent and gay
　　Sat knotting in a shade.

Each slender finger played its part
With such activity and art
As would inflame a youthful heart,
　　And warm the most decayed.

Her fav'rite swain by chance came by,
He saw no anger in her eye;
Yet when the bashful boy drew nigh,
　　She would have seemed afraid.

She let her ivory needle fall,
And hurled away the twisted ball;
But straight gave Strephon such a call
　　As would have raised the dead.

"Dear gentle youth, is't none but thee?
With innocence I dare be free;
By so much truth and modesty
　　No nymph was e'er betrayed.

"Come lean thy head upon my lap;
While thy smooth cheeks I stroke and clap,
Thou mayst securely take a nap":
    Which he, poor fool, obeyed.

She saw him yawn and heard him snore,
And found him fast asleep all o'er;
She sighed and could endure no more,
    But, starting up, she said:

"Such virtue shall rewarded be;
For this thy dull fidelity,
I'll trust thee with my flocks, not me:
    Pursue thy grazing trade.

"Go, milk thy goats and shear thy sheep,
And watch all night thy flocks to keep;
Thou shalt no more be lulled asleep
    By me, mistaken maid."

By the EARL OF DORSET.

ON A LADY[1] WHO FANCIED HERSELF A BEAUTY.

DORINDA'S sparkling wit and eyes,
    United, cast too fierce a light,
Which blazes high but quickly dies,
    Pains not the heart but hurts the sight.

Love is a calmer, gentler joy,
    Smooth are his looks and soft his pace;
Her Cupid is a black-guard boy
    That runs his link full in your face.

By the EARL OF DORSET.

TO CHLORIS FROM THE BLIND ARCHER.

AH, Chloris, 'tis time to disarm your bright eyes
    And lay by those terrible glances;
We live in an age that's more civil and wise
    Than to follow the rules of romances.

When once your round bubbies begin but to pout,
    They'll allow you no long time of courting;
And you'll find it a very hard task to hold out,
    For all maidens are mortal at fourteen.

[1] Catharine Sedley, Countess of Dorchester, mistress of James II.

By the EARL OF DORSET. (A song contributed to SOUTHERNE'S *Sir Antony Love*, 1691.)

IN vain, Clemene, you bestow
    The promised empire of your heart
If you refuse to let me know
    The wealthy charms of every part.

My passion with your kindness grew,
    Tho' beauty gave the first desire:
But beauty only to pursue
    Is following a wand'ring fire.

As hills in perspective suppress
    The free enquiry of the sight;
Restraint makes every pleasure less
    And takes from love the full delight.

Faint kisses may in part supply
    Those eager longings of my soul;
But oh! I'm lost if you deny
    A quick possession of the whole.

By John Wilmot, Earl of
Rochester.

MY dear mistress has a heart
   Soft as those kind looks she gave me,
When, with love's resistless art
   And her eyes, she did enslave me:
But her constancy's so weak,
   She's so wild and apt to wander,
That my jealous heart would break
   Should we live one day asunder.

Melting joys about her move,
   Killing pleasures, wounding blisses;
She can dress her eyes in love,
   And her lips can warm with kisses.
Angels listen when she speaks;
   She's my delight, all mankind's wonder,
But my jealous heart would break,
   Should we live one day asunder.

By the EARL OF ROCHESTER.

GIVE me leave to rail at you,
　I ask nothing but my due;
To call you false and then to say
You shall not keep my heart a day;
But, alas! against my will,
I must be your captive still.
Ah, be kinder then, for I
Cannot change and would not die.

Kindness has resistless charms,
All besides but weakly move;
Fiercest anger it disarms,
And clips the wings of flying love.
Beauty does the heart invade,
Kindness only can persuade;
It gilds the lover's servile chain,
And makes the slaves grow pleased again.

By the Earl of Rochester.

ALL my past life is mine no more,
    The flying hours are gone,
Like transitory dreams given o'er,
Whose images are kept in store
    By memory alone.

The time that is to come is not:
    How can it then be mine?
The present moment's all my lot,
And that, as fast as it is got,
    Phillis, is only thine.

Then talk not of inconstancy,
    False hearts and broken vows;
If I, by miracle, can be
This live-long minute true to thee,
    'Tis all that heaven allows.

By the Earl of Rochester.

As Chloris, full of harmless thought,
    Beneath the willows lay,
Kind Love a comely shepherd brought
    To pass the time away:
She blushed to be encountered so,
    And chid the amorous swain;
But as she strove to rise and go,
    He pulled her back again.

A sudden passion seized her heart
    In spite of her disdain;
She found a pulse in every part,
    And Love in every vein.
"Ah, youth," quoth she, "what charms are these,
    That conquer and surprise?
Ah let me—for, unless you please,
    I have no power to rise."

She faintly spoke and trembling lay,
    For fear he should comply;
Her lovely eyes her heart betray,
    And give her tongue the lie.

Thus she, who princes had denied
    With all their pomp and train,
Was in the lucky minute tried
    And yielded to the swain.[1]

From SIR GEORGE ETHEREGE'S
*The Comical Revenge; or
Love in a Tub*, 1664.

IF she be not as kind as fair,
    But peevish and unhandy,
Leave her, she's only worth the care
    Of some spruce jack-a-dandy.
I would not have thee such an ass,
    Hadst thou ne'er so much leisure,
To sigh and whine for such a lass
    Whose pride's above her pleasure.

LADIES, though to your conquering eyes
    Love owes his chiefest victories,

---

[1] This song was lengthened into a broadside ballad, seven additional stanzas being tacked on. See *Roxburghe Ballads*, ed. J. W. Ebsworth, part xvi., pp. 133-35.

And borrows those bright arms from you
With which he does the world subdue,
 Yet you yourself are not above
 The empire nor the griefs of love.

Then rack not lovers with disdain,
Lest Love on you revenge their pain;
You are not free because you're fair;
The Boy did not his Mother spare:
 Beauty's but an offensive dart,
 It is no armour for the heart.

By Sir George Etherege.

To a very young Lady.

SWEETEST bud of beauty, may
 No untimely frost decay
Th' early glories which we trace
Blooming in thy matchless face.
But kindly opening like the rose
Fresh beauties every day disclose,
Such as by nature are not shown
In all the blossoms she has blown.

And then what conquests shall you make
Who hearts already daily take !
Scorched in the morning with thy beams,
How shall we bear those sad extremes
Which shall attend thy threatening eyes
When thou shalt to thy noon arise ![1]

By Sir George Etherege.

To a Lady, asking him how long he would love her.

It is not, Celia, in our power
   To say how long our love will last ;
It may be we within this hour
May lose those joys we now do taste ;
The blessed, that immortal be,
From change in love are only free.

---

[1] Cf. Waller's verses *To my young Lady Lucy Sidney :—*

"Yet, fairest blossom, do not slight
  That age which you may know so soon :
The rosy morn resigns her light
  And milder glory to the noon :
And then what wonders shall you do,
Whose dawning beauty warms us so !"

Then, since we mortal lovers are,
Ask not how long our love will last;
But while it does, let us take care
Each minute be with pleasure pass'd:
Were it not madness to deny
To live because we're sure to die?

By Sir George Etherege.
(A song contributed to
Nahum Tate's *A Duke
and no Duke*, 1685.)

TELL me no more I am deceived:
   While Silvia seems so kind,
And takes such care to be believed,
   The cheat I fear to find.
To flatter me should falsehood lie
   Concealed in her soft youth,
A thousand times I'd rather die
   Than see the unhappy truth.

My love all malice shall outbrave,
   Let fops in libels rail;
If she the appearances will save,
   No scandal shall prevail.

She makes me think I have her heart:
    How much for that is due?
Tho' she but act the tender part
    The joy she gives is true.

By SIR CAR SCROOPE.[1]

AS Amoret with Phillis sat
    One evening on the plain,
And saw the charming Strephon wait
    To tell the nymph his pain;
The threat'ning danger to remove,
    She whispered in her ear,
"Ah! Phillis, if you would not love,
    This shepherd do not hear;
None ever had so strange an art
    His passion to convey
Into a list'ning virgin's heart
    And steal her soul away:

---

[1] Sir Car Scroope contributed this song to Etherege's *The Man of Mode, or Sir Fopling Flutter*, 1676, for which play he also wrote a prologue. Prefixed to the verses is a note—"Song by Sir C. S." (In the 1722 edition of Sir Charles Sedley's *Works* the song is found, but not in ed. 1702.)

Fly, fly betimes for fear you give
    Occasion for your Fate!"
"In vain," said she, "in vain I strive,
    Alas! 'tis now too late."

From MRS. BEHN'S *Abdelazar,*
or the Moor's Revenge, 1671.

LOVE in fantastic triumph sate
    Whilst bleeding hearts around him flowed,
For whom fresh pains he did create
    And strange tyrannic power he showed.
From thy bright eyes he took his fires,
    Which round about in sport he hurled;
But 'twas from mine he took desires,
    Enough t' undo the amorous world.

From me he took his sighs and tears,
    From thee his pride and cruelty;
From me his languishments and fears,
    And every killing dart from thee.
Thus thou and I the God have armed,
    And set him up a deity;
But my poor heart alone is harmed,
    Whilst thine the victor is and free.

From Mrs. Behn's *The Lucky Chance*, 1687.

O LOVE, that stronger art than wine,
Pleasing delusion, witchery divine,
Want to be prized above all wealth,
Disease that has more joys than health,
Tho' we blaspheme thee in our pain
And of thy tyranny complain,
We all are bettered by thy reign.

What Reason never can bestow
We to this useful Passion owe:
Love wakes the dull from sluggish ease,
And learns a clown the art to please,
Humbles the vain, kindles the cold,
Makes misers free and cowards bold;
'Tis he reforms the sot from drink,
And teaches airy fops to think.
When full brute appetite is fed,
And choked the glutton lies and dead,
Thou new spirits dost dispense
And 'finest the gross delights of sense:
Virtue's unconquerable aid
That against Nature can persuade,

And mak'st a roving mind retire
Within the bounds of just desire;
Cheerer of age, Youth's kind unrest,
And half the heaven of the blest!

By Mrs. Behn.

A THOUSAND martyrs I have made
   All sacrificed to my desire,
A thousand beauties have betrayed
   That languish in resistless fire:
The untamed heart to hand I brought
And fixed the wild and wand'ring thought.

I never vowed nor sighed in vain,
   But both, tho' false, were well received;
The fair are pleased to give us pain,
   And what they wish is soon believed:
And, tho' I talked of wounds and smart,
Love's pleasures only touched my heart.

Alone the glory and the spoil
   I always laughing bore away,
The triumphs without pain or toil,
   Without the hell the heaven of joy:
And while I thus at random rove
Despise the fools that whine for love.

By Mrs. Behn.

O WHAT pleasure 'tis to find
   A coy heart melt by slow degrees !
When to yielding 'tis inclined,
   Yet her fear a ruin sees ;
When her tears do kindly flow
And her sighs do come and go !

O how charming 'tis to meet
   Soft resistance from the fair,
When her pride and wishes meet
   And by turns increase her care ;
O how charming 'tis to know
She would yield but can't tell how !

O how pretty is her scorn
   When, confused 'twixt love and shame,
Still refusing, tho' she burn,
   The soft pressures of my flame !
Her pride in her denial lies
And mine is in my victories.

By Mrs. Behn.

The Invention.[1]

AH he who first found out the way
   Souls to each other to convey
Without dull speaking, sure must be
Something above humanity.
Let the fond world in vain dispute,
And the first mystery impute
Of letters to the learned brood,
And of the glory cheat a god:
'Twas love alone that first the art assayed,
And Psyche was the first fair yielding maid
That was by the dear *billet doux* betrayed.

---

[1] Charles d'Orléans wrote a charming *balade* in praise of the inventor of letter-writing:—

> "Loué soit celui qui trouva
> Premier la manière d'escrire!
> En ce, grand confort ordonna
> Pour amants qui sont en martire;
> Car quand ne peuvent aller dire
> A leurs dames leur grief tourment,
> Ce leur est moult d'alégement,
> Quand par escript peuvent maner
> Les maulx qu'ils portent humblement,
> Pour bien et loyaument amer." &c.

By Mrs. Behn.

The Example.

DAMON, if you'd have me true,
    Be you my precedent and guide:
Example sooner we pursue
    Than the dull dictates of our pride:
Precepts of virtue are too weak an aim,
'Tis demonstration that can best reclaim.

Shew me the path you'd have me go;
    With such a guide I cannot stray:
What you approve, whate'er you do,
    It is but just I bend the way:
If true, my honour favours your design;
If false, revenge is the result of mine.

A lover true, a maid sincere,
    Are to be prized as things divine:
'Tis justice makes the blessing dear,
    Justice of love without design:
And she that reigns not in a heart alone
Is never safe or easy on her throne.

By Mrs. Behn.

OH, how the hand the lover ought to prize
    'Bove any one peculiar grace !
While he is dying for the eyes
    And doting on the lovely face,
The unconsid'ring little knows
How much he to this beauty owes.

That, when the lover absent is,
    Informs him of his mistress' heart ;
'Tis that which gives him all his bliss
    When dear love-secrets 'twill impart :
That plights the faith the maid bestows,
And that confirms the tim'rous vows.

'Tis that betrays the tenderness
    Which the too bashful tongue denies ;
'Tis that which does the heart confess,
    And spares the language of the eyes ;
'Tis that which treasure gives so vast,
Ev'n Iris 'twill to Damon give at last.

By Tom Durfey.

The Winchester Wedding; or Ralph of Reading and Black Bess of the Green.

A T Winchester was a wedding,
    The like was never seen,
'Twixt lusty Ralph of Reading
    And bonny Black Bess of the Green:
The fiddlers were crowding[1] before,
    Each lass was as fine as a queen;
There was a hundred and more,
    For all the country came in:
Brisk Robin led Rose so fair,
    She looked like a lily o' th' vale,
And ruddy-faced Harry led Mary,
    And Roger led bouncing Nell.

With Tommy came smiling Katy,
    He helped her over the stile,
And swore there was none so pretty
    In forty and forty long mile:

[1] Fiddling.

Kit gave a green gown to Betty,
   And lent her his hand to rise;
But Jenny was jeered by Watty
   For looking blue under the eyes:
Thus merrily chatting all,
   They passed to the bride-house along,
With Johnny and pretty-faced Nanny,
   The fairest of all the throng.

The bride came out to meet 'em,
   Afraid the dinner was spoiled;
And ushered 'em in to treat 'em
   With baked and roasted and boiled:
The lads were so frolic and jolly,
   For each had his love by his side,
But Willy was melancholy,
   For he had a mind to the bride:
Then Philip begins her health
   And turns a beer-glass on his thumb;
But Jenkin was reckoned for drinking
   The best in Christendom.

And, now they had dined, advancing
   Into the midst of the Hall,
The fiddlers struck up for dancing
   And Jeremy led up the brawl;

But Margery kept a quarter,
   A lass that was proud of her pelf,
'Cause Arthur had stolen her garter
   And swore he would tie it himself:
She struggled, and blushed, and frowned,
   And ready with anger to cry,
'Cause Arthur, with tying her garter,
   Had slipped his hand too high.

And now, for throwing the stocking,
   The bride away was led;
The bridegroom got drunk and was knocking
   For candles to light 'em to bed:
But Robin, that found him silly,
   Most friendly took him aside,
The while that his wife with Willy
   Was playing at hooper's-hide:
And now the warm game begins,
   The critical minute was come,
And chatting and billing and kissing
   Went merrily round the room.

Pert Stephen was kind to Betty,
   And blithe as a bird in the spring;
And Tommy was so to Katy,
   And married her with a rush-ring:

Sukey, that danced with the cushion,[1]
   An hour from the room had been gone,
And Barnaby knew by her blushing
   That some other dance had been done:
And thus, of fifty fair maids
   That came to the wedding with men,
Scarce five of the fifty was left ye
   That so did return again.

By TOM DURFEY.[2]

THE night her blackest sable wore,
   All gloomy were the skies,
And glittering stars there were no more
   Than those in Stella's eyes;
When at her father's gate I knocked,
   Where I had often been,
And, shrouded only in her smock,
   The fair one let me in.

---

[1] "Cushion-dance" was the name of a dance (a "pretty provocatory dance") used at weddings.

[2] For Durfey's claim to this once popular song see Mr. Ebsworth's *Roxburghe Ballads*, vol. vi. p. 193, &c.

Fast locked within my close embrace,
    She blushing lay ashamed;
Her swelling breasts, and glowing face,
    And every touch inflamed:
My eager passion I obeyed,
    Resolved the fort to win,
And her fond heart was soon betrayed
    To yield and let me in.

Then, then, beyond expressing,
    Immortal was the joy;
I knew no greater blessing,
    So happy then was I:
And she, transported with delight,
    Oft prayed me come again,
And kindly vowed that every night
    She'd rise and let me in.

But ah, at last she proved with bearn,
    And sighing sat, and dull;
And I, who had as much concern,
    Looked then just like a fool:
Her lovely eyes with tears run o'er,
    Repenting her rash sin,
She sighed and cursed that fatal hour
    That e'er she let me in.

But who could cruelly deceive,
    Or from such beauty part?
I loved her so, I could not leave
    The charmer of my heart;
But wedded and concealed the crime,
    Thus all was well again:
And now she thanks the blessed time
    That e'er she let me in.

          By Tom Durfey.

CHLOE'S a nymph in flowery groves,
    A Nereid in the streams;
Saint-like she in the temple moves,
    A woman in my dreams.

Love steals artillery from her eyes,
    The graces point her charms;
Orpheus is rivalled in her voice,
    And Venus in her arms.

Never so happily in one
    Did heaven and earth combine;
And yet 'tis flesh and blood alone
    That makes her so divine.

She looks indeed like other dames,
   With atlas[1] covered o'er;
But when undressed she meets my flames,
   A mortal she's no more.

By Tom Durfey.

YOUNG Philander wooed me long,
   I was peevish and forbad him,
Nor would hear his loving song,
   And yet now I wish I had him;
For each morn I view my glass,
   I perceive the whim is going;
For when wrinkles streak the face
   We may bid farewell to wooing.

Use your time, ye virgins fair,
   Choose before your days are evil;
Fifteen is a season rare,
   Five and forty is the devil:
Just when ripe consent to do't,
   Hug no more the lonely pillow;
Women, like some other fruit,
   Lose their relish when too mellow.

[1] "A silk-satin manufactured in the East."—*Murray*.

By Tom Durfey.

I FOLLOWED fame and got renown,
I ranged all o'er the park and town;
I haunted plays and there grew wise,
Observing my own modish vice;
Friends and wine I next did try,
Yet I found no solid joy;
Greatest pleasures seem too small,
Till Sylvia made amends for all.

But see the state of human bliss,
How vain our best contentment is;
As of my joy she was the chief,
So was she too my greatest grief.
Fate, that I might be undone,
Dooms this angel but for one;
And, alas, too plain I see
That I am not the happy he.

By Tom Durfey.

SOME thirty or forty or fifty at least,
   Or more, I have loved in vain, in vain,
But if you'll vouchsafe to receive a poor guest,
   For once I will venture again, again.

How long I shall be in this mind, this mind,
   Is totally in your own power;
All my days I can pass with the kind, the kind,
   But I'll part with the proud in an hour.

Then if you'll be good-natured and civil, and civil,
   You'll find I can be so too, so too;
But if not you may go, you may go to the devil,
   Or the devil may come to you, to you.

By Tom Durfey.

Kingston Church, a Song.[1]

SWEET, use your time; abuse your time
   No longer, but be wise:
Young lovers now discover you
   Have beauty to be prized;

---

[1] This song was lengthened into a broadside ballad by the addition of seven stanzas. See Mr. Ebsworth's *Roxburghe Ballads*, vol. vi. pp. 139-142.

But if you're coy you'll lose the joy,
   So curst will be the fate;
The flower will fade, you'll die a maid,
   And mourn your chance too late.

At thirteen years and fourteen years
   The virgin's heart may range;
'Twixt fifteen years and fifty years
   You'll find a wondrous change:
Then whilst in tune, in May and June,
   Let love and youth agree,
For if you stay till Christmas day
   The devil shall woo for me.

              From Sir Charles Sedley's
                  The Mulberry Garden,
                  1668.

AH, Chloris, that I now could sit
   As unconcerned as when
Your infant beauty could beget
   No pleasure nor no pain!
When I the dawn used to admire
   And praised the coming day,
I little thought the growing fire
   Must take my rest away.

Your charms in harmless childhood lay
    Like metals in the mine;
Age from no face took more away
    Than youth concealed in thine:
But as your charms insensibly
    To their perfection prest,
Fond Love as unperceived did fly
    And in my bosom rest.

My passion with your beauty grew,
    And Cupid at my heart—
Still as his mother favoured you—
    Threw a new flaming dart.
Each gloried in their wanton part:
    To make a lover, he
Employed the utmost of his art;
    To make a beauty, she.

Though now I slowly bend to love,
    Uncertain of my fate,
If your fair self my chains approve
    I shall my freedom hate.
Lovers, like dying men, may well
    At first disordered be,
Since none alive can truly tell
    What fortune they must see.

By Sir Charles Sedley.

PHILLIS, men say that all my vows
   Are to thy fortune paid;
Alas, my heart he little knows
   Who thinks my love a trade:
Were I of all these woods the lord,
   One berry from thy hand
More solid pleasure would afford
   Than all my large command.
My humble love hath learnt to live
   On what the nicest maid
Without a conscious blush can give
   Beneath the myrtle-shade.[1]
Of costly food it hath no need,
   And nothing will devour,
But like the harmless bee can feed
   And not impair the flower.
A spotless innocence like thine
   May such a flame allow,
Yet thy fair name for ever shine
   As doth thy beauty now.

---

[1] Here the song ends in ed. 1702. The additional verses are found in ed. 1722.

I heard thee wish my lambs might stray
   Safe from the fox's power:
Tho' every one becomes his prey,
   I'm richer than before.

By Sir Charles Sedley.

AURELIA,[1] art thou mad
   To let the world in me
Envy joys I never had
   And censure them in thee?

Filled with grief for what is past,
   Let us at length be wise,
And the banquet boldly taste
   Since we have paid the price.

Love does easy souls despise
   Who lose themselves for toys,
And escape for those devise
   Who taste his utmost joys.

To be thus for trifles blamed
   Like their's a folly is
Who are for vain swearing damned
   And knew no higher bliss.

[1] The text of ed. 1722 is followed. Ed. 1702 gives a somewhat different version.

Love should like the year be crowned
   With sweet variety;
Hope should in the spring be found,
   Kind fears, and jealousy:

In the summer flowers should rise,
   And in the autumn fruit:
His spring doth else but mock our eyes
   And in a scoff salute.

By SIR CHARLES SEDLEY.

CELINDA, think not by disdain
   To vanquish my desire,
By telling me I sigh in vain
   And feed a hopeless fire:
Despair itself too weak does prove
   Your beauty to disarm;
By Fate I was ordained to love
   As you were born to charm.

By Sir Charles Sedley.

PHILLIS, let's shun the common fate,
   And let our love ne'er turn to hate;
I'll dote no longer than I can,
Without being called a faithless man.
When we begin to want discourse,
And kindness seems to taste of force,
As freely as we met we'll part,
Each one possessed of their own heart.
Thus, whilst rash fools themselves undo,
We'll game and give off savers too;
So equally the match we'll make
Both shall be glad to draw the stake.
A smile of thine shall make my bliss,
I will enjoy thee in a kiss:
If from this height our kindness fall,
We'll bravely scorn to love at all:
If thy affection first decay,
I will the blame on Nature lay.
Alas, what cordial can remove
The hasty fate of dying Love?
Thus we will all the world excel
In loving and in parting well.

By Sir Charles Sedley.

To Chloris.

CHLORIS, I cannot say your eyes
    Did my unwary heart surprise;
Nor will I swear it was your face,
Your shape, or any nameless grace;
For, you are so entirely fair,
To love a part injustice were:
No drowning man can know which drop
Of water his last breath did stop:
So when the stars in heaven appear,
And join to make the night look clear,
The light we no one's bounty call,
But the obliging gift of all.
He that does lips or hands adore,
Deserves them only and no more;
But I love all and every part,
And nothing less can ease my heart:
Cupid that lover weakly strikes
Who can express what 'tis he likes.

By Sir Charles Sedley.

NOT,[1] Cælia, that I juster am
    Or better than the rest,
For I would change each hour like them
    Were not my heart at rest;

But I am tied to very thee
    By every thought I have:
Thy face I only care to see,
    Thy heart I only crave.

All that in woman is adored
    In thy dear self I find,
For the whole sex can but afford
    The handsome and the kind.

Why then should I seek farther store
    And still make love anew?
When change itself can give no more
    'Tis easy to be true.

---

[1] In vol. ii., p. 307, of Durfey's *Pills to Purge Melancholy*, 1719, is a copy of verses to Cynthia (by Durfey, I suppose) written in close imitation of this song of Sedley. The poems in vols. i. and ii. of the *Pills* are usually ascribed to Durfey; but some of the pieces in those two volumes are certainly not by him.

By Sir Charles Sedley.

To a devout young Gentlewoman.

Phillis, this early zeal assuage,
 You over-act your part;
The martyrs at your tender age
 Gave Heaven but half their heart.

Old men, till past the pleasure, ne'er
 Declaim against the sin;
'Tis early to begin to fear
 The devil at fifteen.

The world to youth is too severe,
 And, like a treacherous light,
Beauty the actions of the fair
 Exposes to their sight.

And yet this world, as old as 'tis,
 Is oft deceived by't too:
Kind combinations seldom miss,
 Let's try what we can do.

By Sir Charles Sedley.

LOVE still has something of the sea
 From whence his mother rose;
No time his slaves from doubt can free
 Nor give their thoughts repose.

They are becalmed in clearest days,
 And in rough weather tost;
They wither under cold delays
 Or are in tempests lost.

One while they seem to touch the port;
 Then straight into the main
Some angry wind in cruel sport
 The vessel drives again.

At first Disdain and Pride they fear,
 Which if they chance to scape,
Rivals and Falsehood soon appear
 In a more dreadful shape.

By such degrees to joy they come
 And are so long withstood,
So slowly they receive the sum
 It hardly does them good.

'Tis cruel to prolong a pain;
    And to defer a joy,
Believe me, gentle Celemene,
    Offends the winged boy.

An hundred thousand oaths your fears
    Perhaps would not remove;
And if I gazed a thousand years
    I could no deeper love.

By Sir Charles Sedley.

A DIALOGUE BETWEEN AMINTAS AND CELIA.

Celia.

AMINTAS, I am come alone,
    A silly harmless maid:
But whither is thy honour flown?
    I fear I am betrayed:
Thy looks are changed, and in the place
    Of innocent desires,
Methinks I see thy eyes and face
    Glow with unusual fires.

Amintas. Sees not my Celia Nature wear
  One countenance in the spring,
And yet another shape prepare
  To bring the harvest in?
Look on the eagle, how unlike
  He to the egg is found
When he prepares his pounce to strike
  His prey against the ground.
Fears might my infant-love become;
  'Twere want of vigour now,
Should modesty those hopes benumb
  The place and you allow.
Celia. Amintas, hold! what could you worse
  To worst of women do?
Ah how could you a passion nurse
  So much my honour's foe!
Amintas. Make not an idol of a toy
  Which every breath can shake,
Which all must have or none enjoy,
  What course soe'er we take.
Whilst women hate, or men are vain,
  You cannot be secure:
What makes my Celia then a pain
  So needless to endure?

Celia. Could I the world neglect for thee,
  Thy love, tho' dear it cost,
 In some unkind conceit of me
  Would be untimely lost:
 Thou wouldst thy own example fear,
  And every heedless word,
 I chance let fall beyond thy ear,
  Would some new doubt afford.
Amintas. If I am jealous 'tis because
  I know not where you love:
 With me obey Love's gentle laws
  And all my fears remove.
Celia. Women, like things, at second hand
  Do half their value lose;
 But, whilst all courtship they withstand,
  May at their pleasure choose.
Amintas. This were a fine discourse, my dear,
  If we were not alone,
 But now love whispers in my ear
  There's somewhat to be done.

 She said she never would forgive;
  He, kissing, swore she should,
 And told her she was mad to strive
  Against their mutual good.

What further passed I cannot tell,
    But sure not much amiss:
He vowed he loved her dearly well,
    She answered with a kiss.

By Sir Charles Sedley.

SMOOTH was the water, calm the air,
    The evening sun deprest;
Lawyers dismissed the noisy bar,
    The labourer at rest;

When Strephon with his charming fair
    Crossed the proud river Thames,
And to a garden did repair
    To quench their mutual flames.

The crafty waiter soon espied
    Youth sparkling in her eyes;
He brought no ham nor neat-tongues dried,
    But cream and strawberries.

The amorous Strephon asked the maid
    "What's whiter than this cream?"
She blushed and could not tell, she said:
    "Thy teeth, my pretty lamb.

What's redder than these berries are?"
"I know not," she replied:
"Those lips, which I'll no longer spare,"
The burning shepherd cried;

And straight began to hug her:
"This kiss, my dear,
Is sweeter far
Than strawberries, cream, and sugar."

By Sir Charles Sedley.

PHILLIS is my only joy,
 Faithless as the winds or seas;
Sometimes coming, sometimes coy,
 Yet she never fails to please:
  If with a frown
  I am cast down,
  Phillis smiling,
  And beguiling,
Makes me happier than before.

Tho' alas! too late I find
 Nothing can her fancy fix,
Yet the moment she is kind
 I forgive her all her tricks:

Which tho' I see,
I can't get free:
She deceiving,
I believing:
What need lovers wish for more?

By Sir Charles Sedley.

Advice to Lovers.

Damon, if thou wilt believe me,
   'Tis not sighing round the plain;
Songs and sonnets can't relieve thee;
   Faint attempts in love are vain.

Urge but home the fair occasion
   And be master of the field;
To a powerful kind invasion
   'Tis a madness not to yield.

Love gives out a large commission,
   Still indulgent to the brave,
But one sin of base omission
   Never woman yet forgave.

Though she swears she'll ne'er permit ye,
    Cries you're rude and much to blame,
Or with tears implores your pity,
    Be not merciful for shame.

When the fierce assault is over,
    Chloris time enough will find
This her cruel furious lover
    Much more gentle, not so kind.

By Sir Charles Sedley.

On the happy Corydon and Phillis.

YOUNG Corydon and Phillis
    Sat in a lovely grove,
Contriving crowns of lilies,
Repeating toys of love,
    And something else, but what I dare not name.

But as they were a-playing,
She ogled so the swain
It saved her plainly saying
Let's kiss to ease our pain,
    And ———

A thousand times he kist her,
Laying her on the green ;
But as he further prest her
A pretty leg was seen,
    And ――――

So many beauties viewing,
His ardour still increased,
And, greater joys pursuing,
He wandered o'er her breast,
    And ――――

A last effort she trying
His passion to withstand,
Cried, but 'twas faintly crying,
Pray take away your hand,
    And ――――

Young Corydon, grown bolder,
The minutes would improve ;
This is the time, he told her,
To show you how I love,
    And ――――

The nymph seemed almost dying,
Dissolved in amorous heat ;

She kissed and told him, sighing,
My dear, your love is great,
 And ———

But Phillis did recover
Much sooner than the swain;
She blushing asked her lover,
Shall we not kiss again?
 And ———

Thus love his revels keeping,
Till nature at a stand,
From talk they fell to sleeping,
Holding each other's hand,
 And ———

From Sir Charles Sedley's
Bellamira, or the Mistress,
1687.

WHEN first I made love to my Chloris,
 Canon oaths I brought down
  To batter the town,
And I stormed her with amorous stories.

Billets-doux like small shot did ply her,
    And sometimes a song
    Went whizzing along;
But still I was never the nigher.

At last she sent word by a trumpet,
    If I like that life
    She would be my wife,
But never be any man's strumpet.

I told her that Mars would not marry,
    And swore by my scars,
    Single combats and wars,
I'd rather dig stones in a quarry.

By Sir Charles Sedley.

Indifference excused.

LOVE, when 'tis true, needs not the aid
    Of sighs nor oaths to make it known;
And, to convince the cruel'st maid,
    Lovers should use their love alone.

Into their very looks 'twill steal,
   And he that most would hide his flame
Does in that case his pain reveal;
   Silence itself can love proclaim.

This, my Aurelia, made me shun
   The paths that common lovers tread,
Whose guilty passions are begun
   Not in their heart but in their head.

I could not sigh and with crossed arms
   Accuse your rigour and my fate;
Nor tax your beauty with such charms
   As men adore and women hate:

But careless lived and without art,
   Knowing my love you must have spied,
And thinking it a foolish part
   To set to show what none can hide.

From JAMES HOWARD's[1] *The English Monsieur*, 1674.

LADIES, farewell, I must retire:
Though I your faces all admire
And think you heavens in your kinds,
Some for beauties, some for minds;
If I stay and fall in love,
One of these heavens hell would prove.

Could I know one and she not know it,
Perhaps I then might undergo it;
But if the least she guess my mind,
Straight in a circle I'm confined:
By this I see who once doth dote
Must wear a woman's livery coat.

Therefore, this danger to prevent,
And still to keep my heart's content,
Into the country I'll with speed,
With hounds and hawks my fancy feed:
Both safer pleasures to pursue
Than staying to converse with you.

---

[1] James Howard was a brother of Sir Robert Howard (and brother-in-law of Dryden).

From THOMAS SHADWELL'S *A True Widow*, 1678.

A[1] COPY OF VERSES UPON A FLEA PRESENTED TO HIS MISTRESS IN A GOLD CHAIN.

O HAPPY flea, that may'st both kiss and bite,
Like lovers in their height of appetite,
    Her neck so white !
Pretty black alderman in golden chain,
Who suck'st her blood yet put'st her to no pain,
    Whilst I in vain——
    [*Cætera desunt.*]

---

[1] I quote this trifle merely for the whimsical fourth line, "Pretty black alderman in golden chain." In Thomas Heyrick's *Miscellany Poems*, 1691, is a copy of verses by Joshua Barnes, "On a flea presented to a lady, whose breast it had bitten, in a golden wire. 1679":—

  . . . "I saw him surfeit on your lovely breast,
    And snatched the traitor from that precious feast," &c.

From Thomas Shadwell's
The Squire of Alsatia, 1688.

The Expostulation.

"Still wilt thou sigh, and still in vain
    A cold neglectful nymph adore?
No longer fruitlessly complain,
    But to thyself thyself restore.
In youth thou caught'st this fond disease,
    And should'st abandon it in age:
Some other nymph as well may please;
    Absence, or business, disengage."

"On tender hearts the wounds of love,
    Like those imprinted on young trees,
Or kill at first, or else they prove
    Larger b' insensible degrees.
Business I tried, she filled my mind;
    On others' lips my dear I kissed;
But never solid joy could find
    Where I my charming Sylvia missed.

"Long absence, like a Greenland [1] night,
   Made me but wish for sun the more;
And that inimitable light
   She, none but she, could e'er restore."
"She never once regards thy fire,
   Nor ever vents one sigh for thee."
"I must the glorious sun admire
   Though he can never look on me."

"Look well, you'll find she's not so rare;
   Much of her former beauty's gone."
"My love, her shadow, larger far
   Is made by her declining sun.
What if her glories faded be?
   My former wounds I must endure,
For, should the bow unbended be,
   Yet that can never help the cure."

---

[1] Cf. Cowley's verses, *The Parting:*—

"As men in Greenland left beheld the sun
   From their horizon run,
   And thought upon the sad half year
Of cold and darkness they must suffer there,
So on my parting mistress did I look."

By THOMAS OTWAY.

THE ENCHANTMENT.

I DID but look and love a-while,
   'Twas but for one half-hour;
Then to resist I had no will,
   And now I have no power.

To sigh and wish is all my ease;
   Sighs, which do heat impart,
Enough to melt the coldest ice,
   Yet cannot warm your heart.

O would your pity give my heart
   One corner of your breast,
'Twould learn of yours the winning art
   And quickly steal the rest.

MUSA PROTERVA.

By Nahum Tate.

The Penance.

Nymph Fanaret, the gentlest maid
  That ever happy swain obeyed,
(For what offence I cannot say)
A day and night, and half a day,
Banished her shepherd from her sight:
His fault for certain was not slight,
Or sure this tender judge had ne'er
Imposed a penance so severe.
And lest she should anon revoke
What in her warmer rage she spoke,
She bound the sentence with an oath,
Protested by her Faith and Troth,
Nought should compound for his offence
But the full time of abstinence.
Yet when his penance-glass were run,
His hours of castigation done,
Should he defer one moment's space
To come and be restored to grace,
With sparkling threat'ning eyes she swore
That failing would incense her more
Than all his trespasses before.

From *The Westminster Drollery*
(*Second Part*), 1672.

THE AMOROUS GIRL.

THERE'S none so pretty
  As my sweet Betty,
    She bears away the bell;
For sweetness and neatness,
And all completeness,
    All other girls doth excel.

Whenever we meet
She'll lovingly greet
    Me still with a "How d'ye do?"
"Well, I thank you," quoth I:
Then she will reply
    "So am I, sir, the better for you!"

I asked her how;
She told me, not now,
    For walls had ears and eyes;
Nay she bid me take heed
Whatever I did,
  For 'tis good to be merry and wise.

Then I took her by th' hand,
Which she did not withstand,
    And I gave her a smirking kiss;
She gave me another,
Just like the t'other:
    Quoth I, "What a comfort is this!"

This put me in heart
To play o'er my part
    That I had intended before;
But she bid me to hold,
And not be too bold,
    Until she had fastened the door.

Then she went to the hatch
To see that the latch
    And crannies were all cocksure;
And when she had done
She bid me come on,
    For now we were both secure.

And what we did there
I dare not declare,
    But think that silence is best;
And if you will know,
Why, I kissed her, or so,
    But I'll leave you to guess at the rest.

From Thomas Duffett's *New Poems, Songs*, &c., 1676.[1]

Valentine's Day.

BEFORE the youthful spring had dyed
  The earth with Flora's chequered pride,
Before the new-thawed fields were seen
Dressed in a joyful summer's green;
Grey-bearded Winter's frosty chain
Was just dissolved by Phœbus' wain;
And the aspiring God flown high
To guard the spring in 's infancy,
Inviting Flora from her bed
To rob her of her maidenhead:
Ere fair Aurora's blushing head
Had edged the eastern hills with red,
My restless fancy guided me
Into a happy privacy,
Where the embracing trees had made
A pleasant, tho' yet leafless, shade.

[1] This volume is identical with *New Songs and Poems* . . . *By P. W., Gent.* 1677.

Each naked branch in coupling wise
A pretty harmless love-knot ties,
From which conjunction nature shoots
Sweet blossoms and delicious fruits :
The winged music of the air
Did to this amorous grove repair,
And with their tempting notes did grace
The various pleasures of the place.
As I surprised with wonder sate
Each bird chose out his feathered mate,
And seeming fearful of delay
Through yielding air they cut their way;
Some to the woods, some to the groves
To consummate their eager loves.
So have I seen at Hymen's feasts
A company of youthful guests
A thousand ways advance delight;
But when the long-wished lazy night
To bed invokes the blushing bride
Love's endless quarrel to decide,
A silent envy spreads each face,
The men wish his, the maids her place,
And ere that single wedding's o'er
It gives a birth to twenty more.
Musing how pow'rful Nature was,

Sometimes through prickly thorns I pass,
Whose winding branches seemed to court
Me to attend the harmless sport.
Sometimes I walk by crystal springs
Whose gliding streams in circling rings
Unto the music list'ning stood
Till, pressed by the pursuing flood,
Their angry murmurs did betray
How loth they were to pass away.
Grown weary with this pleasing sight
(Excess of pleasure dulls delight),
To rest my drowsy sense, I sought
The softest, sweetest, grassy plot ;
But as I wandered here and there,
A voice arrests my idle ear,
Which from a neighbouring thicket flies.
Drawn thither by my greedy eyes,
Two loving rogues within it lay;
And thus I heard the puppets play.
Long did I muse, but all in vain
What wanton stars that day did reign,
But as my steps did homewards stray
I met my Phœbe by the way,
My Phœbe whose commanding eyes
Had made my heart her sacrifice.

To her fair hand I paid a kiss,
But she returned a greater bliss :
Presenting violets to me,
" Good-morrow, Valentine !" said she.

From *New Airs and Dialogues,*
&c., 1678.

MORE[1] love or more disdain I crave ;
 Sweet, be not still indifferent :
O send me quickly to my grave,
Or else afford me more content.
Or love or hate me more or less,
For Love abhors all lukewarmness.

Give me a tempest if 'twill drive
Me to the place where I would be ;
Or if you'll have me still alive,
Confess you will be kind to me.
Give hopes of bliss or dig my grave :
More love or more disdain I crave.

These words were made
by MR. CHARLES WEBBE.

[1] Set to music by Henry Purcell.

> From *New Airs and Dialogues
> composed for Voices and
> Viols*, 1678.

WHEN[1] I a lover pale do see
    Ready to faint and sickish be,
With hollow eyes, and cheeks so thin
As all his face is nose and chin;
When such a ghost I see in pain
Because he is not loved again,
And pale and faint and sigh and cry;
Oh there's your loving fool! say I.

'Tis love with love should be repaid
And equally on both sides laid;
Love is a load a horse would kill
If it do hang on one side still;
But if he needs will be so fond
As rules of reason go beyond,
And love where he's not loved again,
Faith, let him take it for his pain.

---

[1] Set to music by Henry Purcell.

From *New Airs and Dialogues*,
1678.

MAIDS, beware! maids, beware!
    Nets and traps men's kisses are,
Spread and set merely in wiles,
Baited with oaths, false tears, and smiles.
Fie, away! fie, away!
Indeed you must not: nay, nay, nay!
If I should yield I were undone:
You have your answer, now begone!

By ANNE, MARCHIONESS OF
WHARTON.

HOW hardly I concealed my tears,
    How oft did I complain!
When, many tedious days, my fears
    Told me I loved in vain.

But now my joys as wild are grown,
    And hard to be concealed;
Sorrow may make a silent moan,
    But joy will be revealed.

I tell it to the bleating flocks,
    To every stream and tree;
And bless the hollow murmuring rocks
    For echoing back to me.

Thus you may see with how much joy
    We want, we wish, believe;
'Tis hard such passion to destroy,
    But easy to deceive.

From JOHN PLAYFORD'S *Fifth Book of Choice Airs*, 1684.

"TELL me, Jenny, tell me roundly,
    When will you your heart surrender?
Faith and troth, I love thee soundly,
    'Twas I that was the first pretender.
Ne'er say nay, nor delay,
    Here's my heart and here's my hand too;
All that's mine shall be thine,
    Body and goods at thy command too."

"Ah! how many maids," quoth Jenny,
    Have you promised to be true to?
Fie, I think the devil's in ye [1]
    To kiss a body so as you do.

[1] Old ed. "you."

What d'ye [do]? let me go;
   I can't abide such foolish doing.
Get you gone! naughty man!
   Fie, is this your way of wooing!"

From PHILIP AYRES' *Lyric
Poems, made in imitation
of the Italians,* 1687.

THE MORN.

WHEN light begins the eastern heaven to grace,
And the night's torches to the sun give place,
Diana leaves her shepherd to his sleep,
Grieved that her horns cannot their lustre keep;

The boughs on which the wanton birds do throng
Dance to the music of their chirping song,
Whilst they rejoice the dusky clouds are fled
And bright Aurora rises from her bed;

Then fools and flatterers to courts resort,
Lovers of game up and pursue the sport;
With last night's sleep refreshed, the lab'ring swain
Cheerfully settles to his work again;

Pleased Hob unfolds his flocks, and, whilst they
    feed,
Sits and makes music on his oaten reed:
Then I wake too, and viewing Lesbia's charms
Do glut myself with pleasure in her arms.

By JOHN SHEFFIELD, DUKE
OF BUCKINGHAMSHIRE.

INCONSTANCY EXCUSED.

I MUST confess I am untrue
    To Gloriana's eyes;
But he that's smiled upon by you
    Must all the world despise.

In winter fires of little worth
    Excite our dull desire;
But when the sun breaks kindly forth
    Those fainter flames expire.

Then blame me not for slighting now
    What I did once adore:
O do but this one change allow,
    And I can change no more;

Fixt by your never-failing charms
    Till I with age decay,
Till languishing within your arms
    I sigh my soul away.

By JOHN SHEFFIELD, DUKE
  OF BUCKINGHAMSHIRE.

COME, Celia, let's agree at last
    To love and live in quiet;
Let's tie the knot so very fast
    That time shall ne'er untie it.
Love's dearest joys they never prove,
    Who free from quarrels live;
'Tis sure a godlike part of love
    Each other to forgive.

When least I seemed concerned I took
    No pleasure, nor had rest;
And when I feigned an angry look,
    Alas! I loved you best.
Say but the same to me, you'll find
    How blest will be our fate;
Sure to be grateful, to be kind,
    Can never be too late.

By William Congreve.

TELL me no more I am deceived,
    That Chloe's false and common;
By Heaven! I all along believed
    She was a very woman;
As such I liked, as such caressed,
She still was constant,—when possessed:
    She could do more for no man.

But oh! her thoughts on others ran,
    And that you think a hard thing?
Perhaps she fancied you the man?
    Why, what care I one farthing?
You think she's false, I'm sure she's kind,
I'll take her body, you her mind:
    Who has the better bargain?

By WILLIAM CONGREVE.

PIOUS Selinda[1] goes to prayers
    If I but ask the favour;
And yet the tender fool's in tears
    When she believes I'll leave her.

Would I were free from this restraint,
    Or else had hopes to win her;
Would she could make of me a saint,
    Or I of her a sinner!

By WILLIAM CONGREVE.

FAIR Amoret is gone astray,
    Pursue and seek her every lover;
I'll tell the signs by which you may
    The wand'ring shepherdess discover.

Coquet and coy at once her air,
    Both studied, tho' both seem neglected;
Careless she is with artful care,
    Affecting to seem unaffected.

[1] Mrs. Bracegirdle.

With skill her eyes dart ev'ry glance,
  Yet change so soon you'd ne'er suspect 'em;
For she'd persuade they wound by chance,
  Tho' certain aim and art direct 'em.

She likes herself, yet others hates
  For that which in herself she prizes;
And while she laughs at them, forgets
  She is the thing that she despises.

From JOHN WILSON'S *Belphegor*, 1690.

WERE I to take wife,
    As 'tis for my life,
She should be brisk, pleasant, and merry;
    A lovely fine brown,
    A face all her own,
With a lip red and round as a cherry.

    Not much of the wise,
    Less of the precise,
Nor over-reserved, nor yet flying;
    Hard breasts, a straight back,
    An eye full and black,
But languishing as she were dying.

And then for her dress,
Be't more or be't less,
Not tawdry set out nor yet meanly;
And one thing beside,
Just, just so much pride
As may serve to keep honest and cleanly.

By ANNE FINCH, COUNTESS
OF WINCHILSEA.

PERSUADE me not there is a grace
   Proceeds from Silvia's voice or lute,
Against Miranda's charming face
   To make her hold the least dispute.

Music, which tunes the soul for love
   And stirs up all our soft desires,
Does but the growing flame improve
   Which pow'rful Beauty first inspires.

Thus, whilst with art she plays and sings,
   I to Miranda, standing by,
Impute the music of the strings
   And all the melting words apply.

From Thomas Southerne's
Sir Antony Love, 1691.

PURSUING beauty, men descry
    The distant shore and long to prove
(Still richer in variety)
    The treasures of the land of love.

We women, like weak Indians, stand,
    Inviting, from our golden coast,
The wand'ring rovers to our land:
    But she who trades with 'em is lost.

With humble vows they first begin,
    Stealing, unseen, into the heart;
But, by possession settled in,
    They quickly act another part.

For beads and baubles we resign
    In ignorance our shining store;
Discover nature's richest mine,
    And yet the tyrants will have more.

Be wise, be wise, and do not try
    How he can court or you be won,
For love is but discovery:
    When that is made the pleasure's done.

By GEORGE GRANVILLE, LORD
LANSDOWNE.

TO MIRA.

WHY, cruel creature, why so bent
   To vex a tender heart?
To gold and title you relent;
   Love throws in vain his dart.

Let glittering fools in courts be great,
   For pay let armies move:
Beauty should have no other bait
   But gentle vows and love.

If on those endless charms you lay
   The value that's their due,
Kings are themselves too poor to pay,
   A thousand worlds too few:

But if a passion without vice,
   Without disguise or art,
Ah, Mira, if true love's your price,
   Behold it in my heart.

By Lord Lansdowne.

CHLOE'S the wonder of her sex,
   'Tis well her heart is tender:
How might such killing eyes perplex,
   With virtue to defend her!

But Nature, graciously inclined
   With liberal hand to please us,
Has to her boundless beauty joined
   A boundless bent to ease us.

By Lord Lansdowne.

Chloe.

IMPATIENT with desire, at last
   I ventured to lay forms aside:
'Twas I was modest, not she chaste:
   Chloe, so gently pressed, complied.

With idle awe, an am'rous fool,
   I gazed upon her eyes with fear:
Say, Love, how came your slave so dull
   To read no better there?

Thus to ourselves the greatest foes,
    Altho' the nymph be well inclined,
For want of courage to propose,
    By our own folly she's unkind.

By LORD LANSDOWNE.

CORINNA.

SO well Corinna likes the joy,
    She vows she'll never more be coy,
She drinks eternal draughts of pleasure :
    Eternal draughts do not suffice,
" O ! give me, give me more," she cries,
" 'Tis all too little, little measure."

Thus wisely she makes up for time
Misspent, while youth was in its prime :
So travellers who waste the day,
Careful and cautious of their way,
Noting at length the setting sun
They mend their pace as night comes on,
Double their speed to reach their inn,
And whip and spur through thick and thin.

By Tom Brown.

To[1] charming Cælia's arms I flew,
    And there all night I feasted;
No god such transport ever knew,
    Or mortal ever tasted.

Lost in the sweet tumultuous joy,
    And blessed beyond expressing,
"How can your slave, my fair," said I,
    "Reward so great a blessing?

"The whole creation's wealth survey,
    O'er both the Indies wander;
Ask what bribed senates give away,
    And fighting monarchs squander;

---

[1] An imitation of the following epigram of Martial (xii. 65):—

"Formosa Phillis nocte cum mihi tota
Se præstitisset omnibus modis largam,
Et cogitarem mane quod darem munus,
Utrumne Cosmi, Nicerotis an libram,
An Bæticarum pondus acre lanarum,
An de moneta Cæsaris decem flavos:
Amplexa collum basioque tam longo
Blandita, quam sunt nuptiæ columbarum,
Rogare cœpit Phillis amphoram vini."

"The richest spoils of earth and air,
  The rifled ocean's treasure:
'Tis all too poor a bribe by far
  To purchase so much pleasure."

She blushing cried, "My life, my dear,
  Since Cælia thus you fancy,
Give her—but 'tis too much, I fear,—
  A rundlet of right Nantzy."

By WILLIAM WALSH.

UPON A FAVOUR OFFERED.

CÆLIA, too late you would repent:
  The off'ring all your store
Is now but like a pardon sent
  To one that's dead before.

While at the first you cruel proved,
  And grant the bliss too late,
You hindered me of one I loved
  To give me one I hate.

I thought you innocent as fair
   When first my court I made ;
But when your falsehoods plain appear
   My love no longer stayed.

Your bounty of those favours shown,
   Whose worth you first deface,
Is melting valued metals down
   And giving us the brass.

Oh since the thing we beg's a toy
   That's prized by love alone,
Why cannot women grant the joy
   Before our love is gone?

By WILLIAM WALSH.

THE DESPAIRING LOVER.

DISTRACTED with care
   For Phillis the fair,
Since nothing could move her,
Poor Damon, her lover,
Resolves in despair
No longer to languish
Nor bear so much anguish ;

But, mad with his love,
   To a precipice goes,
Where a leap from above
   Would soon finish his woes.

When in rage he came there,
Beholding how steep
The sides did appear,
And the bottom how deep;
His torments projecting,
And sadly reflecting
That a lover forsaken
   A new love may get,
But a neck when once broken
   Isn't easily set;

And that he could die
Whenever he would,
But that he could live
But as long as he could:
How grievous soever
The torment might grow,
He scorned to endeavour
To finish it so;

And bold, unconcerned
    At thoughts of the pain,
He calmly returned
    To his cottage again.

By Bishop Atterbury.

Written on a White Fan borrowed from Miss Osborne, afterwards his wife.

FLAVIA the least and slightest toy
    Can with resistless art employ:
This fan in meaner hands would prove
An engine of small force in love;
Yet she with graceful air and mien,
Not to be told or safely seen,
Directs its wanton motions so
That it wounds more than Cupid's bow;
Gives coolness to the matchless dame,
To every other breast—a flame.

By John Oldmixon.

The Grove.

O 'TIS sweet, 'tis wondrous sweet
When I and Amaryllis meet
In a fragrant shady grove,
Full of wishes, full of love.
O what pretty things we say!
How the minutes fly away!
When, with glances mingling kisses,
We prepare for softer blisses;
On some mossy bank we lie,
Play and touch, embrace and die;
Then from little feuds and jars
We proceed to amorous wars;
O how many heavens we find!
I am young and she is kind,
Kind and free without design,
Mine at will and only mine;
Smiling always, always toying,
Ever fond, yet never cloying.
Could the coldest hermit see
Half the sweets enjoyed by me;

Happy once to see her eyes,
Press her lips and hear her sighs,
Clasp her waist and touch her skin,
Soon he would forget the sin:
All his darling hopes of bliss
In a distant Paradise,
All with ease he would resign
For a minute's taste of mine.

By JOHN OLDMIXON.

TO CHLOE.

PRITHEE, Chloe, not so fast,
   Let's not run and wed in haste;
We've a thousand things to do;
You must fly and I pursue,
You must frown and I must sigh,
I intreat and you deny.
Stay—if I am never crost,
Half the pleasure will be lost.
Be, or seem to be, severe;
Give me reason to despair:
Fondness will my wishes cloy,
Make me careless of the joy.

Lovers may of course complain
Of their trouble and their pain,
But, if pain and trouble cease,
Love without it will not please.

By JOHN OLDMIXON.

WHEN with Flavia I am toying
    She with little sports gives o'er;
Kissing is not half enjoying,
    Youth and passion covet more.
Every touch, methinks, should move her
    And to dearer joys invite,
When she knows how much I love her
    And is fond of the delight.

Oh I see her young and tender,
    Feel her lips with passion warm,
See her ready to surrender
    When her fears dissolve the charm!
Banish, Flavia, all suspicion,
    All your sullen doubts destroy:
Trust me, there's no worse condition
    Than to wish and not enjoy.

By John Oldmixon.

THOSE arts which common beauties move,
    Corinna, you despise:
You think there's nothing wise in love
    Or eloquent in sighs.
You laugh at ogle, cant, and song,
    And promises abuse:
But say—for I have courted long—
    What methods shall I use?

We must not praise your charms and wit,
    Nor talk of dart and flame;
But sometimes you can think it fit
    To smile at what you blame.
Your sex's forms, which you disown,
    Alas! you can't forbear;
But in a minute smile and frown,
    Are tender and severe.

Corinna, let us now be free;
    No more your arts pursue,
Unless you suffer me to be
    As whimsical as you.

At last the vain dispute desist,
   To love resign the field:
'Twas custom forced you to resist,
   And custom bids you yield.

By PETER ANTHONY MOTTEUX.

MAN is for the woman made,
   And the woman made for man;
As the spur is for the jade,
As the scabbard for the blade,
As for digging is the spade,
As for liquor is the can,
So man is for the woman made
And the woman made for man.

As the sceptre's to be swayed,
As for night's the serenade,
As for pudding is the pan
And to cool us is the fan,
So man is for the woman made
And the woman made for man.

Be she widow, wife, or maid,
Be she wanton, be she staid,
Be she well or ill arrayed,
Whore, bawd, or harridan,
Yet man is for the woman made
And the woman made for man.

By PETER ANTHONY MOTTEUX.

I LOVE, but she alone shall know,
   Who is herself my treasure:
Vain lovers when their joys they show
   Call partners to their pleasure:
Let empty beaux the favour miss
   While they would have it known;
That soul's too narrow for the bliss
   Who can't enjoy alone.

Then never let my love be told
   By way of modern toasting;
The sweetest joy, like fairy gold,
   Is lost by selfish boasting.
Too rich to show, what I profess,
   My treasure I'll conceal;
I may my pains of love confess,
   But ne'er my joys reveal.

By Peter Anthony Motteux.

Boasting fops, who court the fair
   For the fame of being loved,
You who daily prating are
   Of the hearts your charms have moved,
Still be vain in talk and dress,
   But, while shadows you pursue,
Own that some who boast it less
   May be blest as much as you.

Love and birding are allied,
   Baits and nets alike they have,
The same arts in both are tried
   The unwary to enslave:
If in each you'd happy prove,
   Without noise still watch your prey;
For, in birding and in love,
   While we talk it flies away.

By Thomas Rymer.

A Kind Man to his Froward Mate.

PHILLIS, I expect caresses,
    Lay that angry vizard by;
I know better what the face is
That obtained the victory
And first made a slave of me:
'Twas adorned with all the Graces,
Which from this affrighted flee.

Never labour to unsettle,
Never strive where Fates ordain;
In a sort of stubborn metal
Linked together we remain:
Trust me, Phillis, 'tis in vain,
'Tis unwise to make it rattle,
When we cannot break the chain.

By the huff, the heat, the clamour,
Surely Vulcan's forge is near,
Where Jove's angry bolts they hammer;
Love no shafts has pointed here,
'Tis too hot for Love to bear:
Bless me, if e'er this enamour!
Phillis, pray this heat forbear.

This is fire to burn a city;
Give us Love's kind, gentle flame,
Where two hearts, in mutual treaty,
All by-wandering thoughts reclaim,
Every spark of discord tame,
And, o'erwhelmed with amorous pity,
Pant and melt and glow[1] the same.

By THOMAS RYMER.

LATE when Love I seemed to slight,
Phillis smiled, as well she might.
"Now," said she, "our throne may tremble,
Men our province now invade;
Men take up our royal trade;
Men, even men, do now dissemble:
In the dust our Empire's laid."

Tutored by the wise and grave,
Loath was I to be a slave:
Mistress sounded arbitrary,

---

[1] Old ed. "grow."

So I chose to hide my flame;
Friendship a discreeter name:
But she scorns one jot to vary,
She will Love or nothing claim.

Be a lover, or pretend,
Rather than the warmest friend:
Friendship of another kind is,
Swedish coin of gross allay,
A cart-load will scarce defray:
Love, one grain, is worth the Indies,
Only Love is current pay.

From GEORGE FARQUHAR'S
The Constant Couple, 1700.

THUS Damon knocked at Celia's door,
He sighed and begged and wept and swore:
    The sign was so: [*Knocks.*
    She answered "No,
    No, no, no."   [*Knocks thrice.*
Again he sighed, again he prayed:
"No, Damon, no, I am a maid;

   Consider,
    No,
   I'm a maid.
    No," &c.
At last his sighs and tears made way;
She rose and softly turned the key:
" Come in," said she, " but do not stay;
   I may conclude
   You will be rude:
But, if you are, you may."

www.ingramcontent.com/pod-product-compliance
Lightning Source LLC
Chambersburg PA
CBHW030345170426
43202CB00010B/1252